NEIGHBORS

Muslims in North America

Interviews by Elias D. Mallon

Friendship Press • New York

© 1989 by Friendship Press
Editorial Offices:
475 Riverside Drive, Room 772, New York, NY 10115
Distribution Offices:
P.O. Box 37844, Cincinnati, OH 45222-0844

Manufactured in the United States of America
93 92 91 90 89   5 4 3 2 1

Library of Congress Cataloging in Publication Data

Mallon, Elias D., 1944–
    Neighbors : Muslims in North America.

    1. Islam — United States.   2. Islam — Canada.
3. Muslims — United States — Interviews.   4. Muslims —
Canada — Interviews.   I. Title.
BP67.A1M35   1989   305.6'971071   89-1406
ISBN 0-377-00198-8

Contents

To my parents
Genevieve and Donald Mallon

Introduction

Muslim. Islam. The words evoke powerful images in the minds of Canadians and Americans whether they are actively religious or not. Among those relatively familiar with Islam, the images often recall the accomplishments of Islam's past — the great cultures of the Baghdad of *A Thousand and One Nights,* of the Moghuls in India and of the Ottoman Empire in Turkey. Among those less familiar with Islam, the images often elicit visions of exotic, religious fanatics ready to kill any and all who oppose them.

Recent events have, if anything, strengthened the negative image of Islam and Muslims in the eyes of the West. A group that calls itself the Islamic Jihad has kidnapped several citizens of Western countries. In the minds of millions of people the word *ayatollah* has taken on connotations that it never originally bore and that do not describe the attitudes and ways of life of the vast majority of ayatollahs. And so the negative, fearful image of Islam not only endures, it grows in the minds of many.

1

Muslim. Islam. These words evoke powerful images in the minds of Canadians and Americans. Some of these images are outdated, some are simply wrong, most are built on little or no personal experience. One image that "Muslim" and "Islam" do not evoke is that of neighbor. When we hear the names of other ethnic or religious groups, our minds often picture someone we know who belongs to that group. While we may have opinions about and even prejudices towards the group as a whole, those opinions and prejudices are moderated by friendship and neighborliness. Prejudices begin to break down when a person begins to realize that not everyone in a group fits the image. Prejudices break down further when a person becomes a good neighbor or a friend to someone who belongs to a minority group that suffers from "bad press" or prejudice.

Neighbors is an attempt to help people create new images. It seeks to introduce readers not so much to Islam as to Muslims: the Muslim who lives next door; the Muslim at work; the Muslim at school with my children. True, Islam exists as a major religion; indeed, it is the main religion in many countries and cultures that seem exotic to us. But Islam is also the religion of a housewife of Norwegian and English descent in Los Angeles. It is the religion of a young woman studying philosophy at UCLA. It is the religion of a cardiologist in New Jersey. Islam is a world religion — and it is part of the religious reality of the United States and Canada. To some extent, this reality is becoming visible as the skylines of North American cities are reshaped by an increasing number of mosques. But buildings rarely contribute to mutual understanding. It takes personal contact for mutual understanding.

Neighbors is an attempt to introduce readers to "the Muslim next door." By seeing the concerns, the hopes and experiences of nine people, men and women of different ages, ethnic and educational backgrounds, readers have the opportunity to get to know Muslims who live literally next door. It is my hope that as you get to know the Muslims in this book, you will also feel more comfortable about getting to know the Muslim who works as your colleague or who lives in your neighborhood.

Islam is a world religion. It is important that Americans and Canadians be familiar with and knowledgeable about it as a world religion. But Islam is first and foremost a religion of people, believers. Knowledge of any religion is incomplete if it does not also increase our familiarity with the people to whom that religion brings transformation, consolation and ultimate meaning. We begin truly to understand a religion when we have a friend who is a follower of that religion. *Neighbors* is my attempt to introduce Christians not only to Islam but more especially to Muslims, in the hope that "Muslim" and "Islam" will evoke images of people with names, images of neighbors and friends.

1

Mary Lahaj

*Mary Lahaj is a mother and a scholar of Leba-
nese descent. She is a graduate student in Islamic
Studies at Hartford Theological Seminary. Ms.
Lahaj is an active member of the Islamic Center
in Quincy, Massachusetts. She has a full sched-
ule raising her young son, working at the Islamic
Center and completing her studies.*

Mary Lahaj: I am an American and I was born here.
I live in Weymouth, Massachusetts. My parents were
born here and my grandparents came from Lebanon —
on both sides of the family. On one side of the family,
my father's side, they came from Baalbek; and on the
other side they came from Tripoli, but not in the city, in

the mountains. My grandfather came here and I suspect he was here for about seventy-five years.

Elias Mallon: So your family has been in the United States for quite awhile. You said that your grandparents came from Baalbek and from Tripoli. Are they Sunni or Shi'ite?[1]

ML: Sunni.

EM: Tell me a little about your family.

ML: It was about 1930 when my mother's father, Haj Muhammad Omar, came here and saw that the Muslims were not practicing their religion, so he said we need a mosque. And his family and my father's family and three or four other families became the nucleus of this project. They formed the Arab American Banner Society, and they started to raise funds. It took them thirty years to build the first mosque. It was finally built in 1964. So I'm very proud that both my families have been involved in the establishment of this community.

Elias: And your profession?

---

[1]Sunnis represent perhaps ninety percent of the Islamic community. The name derives from the *sunna*, the example set by the Prophet Muhammad. *Sunni* is the singular form of the noun derived from *sunna*; as a convenience in English, the plural is formed by adding an "s." In Arabic, *Shi'a* is a plural noun meaning "partisans" or "followers" of the Prophet's household. The Shi'a are Muslims who believe that leadership should come from descendants of Muhammad's family. Because the Arabic singular is difficult for English speakers to pronounce, a single member of the Shi'a branch of Islam is often called a Shi'ite. "Shi'ite" is also used as an adjective, as is "shi'i," a transliteration closer to the Arabic adjective.

ML: Well, right at the moment I am a graduate student. I study at the Hartford Seminary, Hartford, Connecticut. Islamic Studies and Christian-Muslim relations, a Master's Degree.

EM: Could you describe the spiritual journey that you went through that brought you where you are now as a Muslim woman?

ML: When I was growing up my family held their religion to be very important, but they were selective about their practices, their obligations. I didn't see them pray; they didn't teach us to speak Arabic. They spoke it among themselves in private conversation. But still they maintained what they knew in their heart. They could read the Qur'an and so it was important, but it was not transmitted to me through education. They didn't have much education; they were born Muslim. And I didn't have any education in Islam. So what was transmitted to me was that I didn't eat pork,[2] I didn't drink and that Jesus (PBUH[3]) was not crucified on a cross. And this was all I knew about religion. Period. That's my spiritual journey.

So what happened? By the time I was fifteen, I was socialized to American culture. I felt isolated, I felt alone. I didn't know how to pray so I couldn't commune with God about this. I thought my mother was eccentric. The

---

[2]Dietary requirements in Islam are based on interpretations of verses in the Qur'an that forbid the eating of carrion, blood and the meat of swine and of any animal not slaughtered in the name of God and the drinking of alcoholic beverages. The prohibition of alcohol is held to include drugs.

[3]PBUH, an abbreviation for "peace be upon him." This exclamation is used by Muslims after mentioning the names of one of the prophets.

only other people that were like me were my cousins, and they really didn't matter in the sense that the world mattered. Inside my house it was an invisible culture, an invisible religion. Outside was everything for me. And as soon as the mosque was built, when I was fifteen years old, my relatives said to me, "Go to the mosque and learn how to pray." And I didn't like that at all. So I resisted that. And they didn't go themselves because they were fighting with their relatives.

I went away to college at the University of Massachusetts at Amherst. I graduated in 1970, and I didn't come back here. I stopped fasting during the fast of Ramadan,[4] which was one thing we all did. As soon as I left the house, that was my last connection with what little bit of Islam I had. And I really became like a slave to society. Whatever society's values were, they were my values. Whatever the morals were, they were my morals. I was a slave to Madison Avenue, to the fashion industry, to the entertainment industry. I believed in romance and love. I bought everything hook, line and sinker. I had no idea that there was anything wrong with it. I always say to my mother, "You didn't teach me about Islam; I went astray." And she always says to me, "You did exactly what you wanted to do." All I know is that it was a kind of tyranny. I was enslaved, just beaten down to the ground. I finally fell to my knees in 1978 and asked God to help me. I don't think I had thought of God for twenty years. And I asked God to help me. And you know once you ask God to help you, He helps you. And I went to a film and the whole thing started to happen.

EM: Where did you go?

---

[4]The ninth month of the Muslim year, spent in fasting from sunrise to sunset.

ML: To a movie. I was living in New York City at the time. I went to see *Al-rasul*, The Message. Muslims were protesting outside, saying it was against their religion to sell religion and that they were going to blow up the theatre. And my Iranian girl friend and I went in to watch the movie. I was converted! I saw this movie, the history, the heritage, the pride and the pain. The pain. I could really identify with the pain and struggling. And you know, I got four dollars worth of religion from that movie. And it just turned my head around. I became fascinated by how much there was that I knew nothing about. Absolutely nothing. I wanted to change, to better myself, to improve my life. And I turned off one path onto another. This was my spiritual watershed.

Slowly I began to study. I wasn't interested in the Qur'an. Some people just open the Qur'an and they become converted. I never did that. And I call myself a born-again Muslim. I just began to read books about Islam. What interested me was the social aspect, because I was such a sucker for this society. I almost thought I was a Christian, but you don't want to attribute all the values and the lack of values and all the bad things in society to Christianity or to Judaism. Whatever the society is I was. You know, I was like those people. All those people...*kafir*. I was a *kafir*.[5] And I believed in everything — the music, the clothes, everything. I wanted it all, tried it all. And maybe this is what we do when we're young.

My introduction to Islam was books about law and the *hadith*, the Prophet's *sunna*.[6] For example, "A Mus-

---

[5]*Kafir*, i.e., an unbeliever, someone who denies the truth of God.

[6]*Hadith* and *sunna* are both essential to Islam. *Hadith* consists of accounts of the sayings, decisions and actions of Muhammad. *Sunna*, a more general term that means "a path," refers to the way Muhammad behaved and acted during his life.

lim is a person who would never harm anyone with his tongue or with his hand." You should always feel that way. And faith. You do not have real faith until you want for others what you want for yourself. There are common ideals that peoples of all faiths strive towards. I was shown by the sunna and the Prophet's example and God's will.

EM: How did you get reinvolved with the mosque here in Quincy?

ML: My aunt was working as the secretary here. And she wanted to retire and move to Missouri to live with her daughter. I had just had my baby, my little boy, and I was looking for a job where I could have him with me and work. He's used to me carrying on; he's become accustomed to keeping himself busy while I do other things. So she passed the job to me. It was a wonderful opportunity and I've been working with people like the imam[7] and Dr. Karim Kudeiry, the president of this center. I wish you could meet him. Working with people like this has been a tremendous education.

EM: How long have you been working here?

ML: It will be four years in August.

EM: In your everyday life how do you express your identity as a Muslim?

---

[7] A Muslim prayer leader. For the Shi'a, the Imam is a religious leader who is a special representative of the Prophet Muhammad. Shi'i Imams have appeared, according to various traditions, at definite times in history and are not to be confused with the imams who lead prayers at mosques throughout the Muslim world.

ML: By praying, by fasting, by paying the *zakat*.

EM: Many of the people who will be reading this book will not know the meaning of the *zakat*. Could you explain it for us?

ML: I'll do my best. The *zakat* is not a charity where you give what you feel like and when you feel like. The *zakat* is an obligation upon all Muslims to pay 2½ percent of their holdings — in other words, of the money they have accumulated at the end of the year, after they've paid everything that they have to pay. From that money they need to take 2½ percent of goods or valuables, gold, whatever commodities they have. Or just their cash in the bank. They have to give that annually for the poor.

EM: And so that would be one of the ways that you express your identity.

ML: In this country I think that probably the most salient way of expressing my identity is with my head cover.

EM: We'll come back to that. How do you feel you are perceived as a Muslim or how Islam is perceived by non-Muslims that you know professionally or socially?

ML: People relate to people as persons. And we are people and not just our religion. The quality of Islam that I have tried to understand in these last ten years is that religion is your manners. It's how good you are to your brother; it's how considerate you are, how much you control your temper; it's not making jokes and not making fun of people or talking behind their backs.

And these are things that we learned from the Prophet's sunna and from the Qur'an. When you work or socialize with people they know you for who you are and Islam makes you a better person.

EM: What kind of reactions do you encounter when people meet you the first time, from people who know that you're a Muslim woman?

ML: For most people this head cover signals that you're from another country. They don't even think that it's your religion. So I say that it's my religion. They ask, "Why do you cover your head?" I say because it's my religion. The other stereotypes that I have had to deal with — in particular from my own brothers — is that Islam is backward.

EM: Are your brothers practicing Muslims?

ML: Oh, no. They've never read a single book about Islam. They don't know anything about it. They don't know how to pray. They only know the *Fatihah*.[8] So they've bought the stereotype as much as anyone else.

EM: It's very interesting that one of the stereotypes comes from your own family.

ML: That's right. Well, there are not a lot of people in my family like me. I'm the only one. I mean, cousins, brothers, sisters, aunts, uncles. My mother doesn't cover her head. In fact, she tells me, "Take that rag off your head. If you're going out for an interview take that rag off your head!" She doesn't support this.

---

[8]The *Fatihah* is the opening chapter of the Qur'an. As such, it numbers among the most frequent prayers prayed by Muslims.

EM: How do people react to you when they see you? If you're going for an interview, they may have one idea in mind because of your education. And then you're quite different from the idea they've had. Have you had any reactions like that? Good or bad?

ML: I've had experience going around without the cover for many years — and then trying to put the cover on. It took three years to get it on and keep it on. You have to get used to it. You know, your vanity, the days your hair looks beautiful. You have to try to adjust. The reaction from people, people in stores, people wherever I have to do business, has been that they are more trusting, more considerate. I don't know, it sort of brings out something good in them. It touches them somehow. Very few people look strangely at me. Most people feel comfortable once they talk to you. And if you're comfortable, they're comfortable. Even if they don't know what you are or who you are, you can still be comfortable. I've had a lot of acquaintances who have gone on in their ignorance about Islam for long, long periods of time before they would ever ask questions.

EM: What would you see as important issues for Muslims in North America today?

ML: Education. Educating our children. Getting our children out of the school system, which is just not adequate. Political power. Giving our children some political power as well as education. Why should they be politically impotent, if we can give them some political power? And making some kind of an impact on this society that would be of benefit to our fellow people.

2

Muhammad Z. Pirzada

Muhammad Pirzada is a native of Pakistan. Educated in Pakistan and Britain, Mr. Pirzada is a combustion engineer, whose expertise is air pollution control. He is also active in promoting interfaith cooperation in the New York area.

Elias Mallon: Where do you and your family come from originally?

Muhammad Z. Pirzada: Originally my family comes from India. But we emigrated to Pakistan in 1947 when the partition took place between India and Pakistan.

EM: Where in India?

MZP: We are from a village about seventy miles from New Delhi. The grave of my grandfather is there. My forefathers have the same name as this village. But basically my name is Pirzada. *Sha* and *pir* mean "religious people." We are a very religious family.

EM: How old were you when you went to Pakistan?

MZP: I think I was four years old.

EM: How long did you live in Pakistan?

MZP: I got my basic education there. I got my Bachelor's degree in Karachi. Then I went to England and I studied in London. I got my professional education in engineering. I am a scientist — or almost a scientist. Then I went back to Pakistan and did some research work.

EM: Describe to me the cultural setting of the place where you lived in Pakistan.

MZP: I come from Karachi. But I also would go to the Sind area where there was some open land. And so I had some interaction with both the city and the country.

EM: How long have you lived in North America?

MZP: I came here in 1977.

EM: So, eleven years. Tell me about your family.

MZP: I belong to a family called the Pirzadas. These are the people who teach Islam; they are religious teachers. And I come from that family. It is very well known in India. My father was a doctor, a teacher, a professional.

EM: At what level did he teach?

MZP: High school. He taught religion. He had a very good command of Persian and Arabic.

EM: What is your family now? Are you married? Do you have children?

MZP: Yes, I am married and I have four sons. Two sons are at college. The oldest one was born in London and the other three in Karachi.

EM: Was religion important in your family when you were growing up?

MZP: It was important. We practiced the prayer five times a day, the recitation of the Holy Qur'an in the morning, going to the *jum'ah*,[1] the prayers of the congregation, and to gatherings and lectures at home. And all the festivities. We were constantly involved.

EM: Karachi is a Muslim city. Were there a lot of mosques near your home?

MZP: Yes. Practically every small neighborhood has a mosque. For every forty and fifty homes you will find a mosque.

EM: Did your family perform the five prayers every day?

---

[1]*Jum'ah* is the Friday congregational prayer, which is usually observed in a mosque.

MZP: Oh, yes, my mother, my father, my sisters and my brothers. I remember when I was six or seven I would see sunup and I would say, "Why didn't you wake me up? I wanted to join you in the prayers." I used to cry and say to my mother, "Why don't you wake me up in the morning?" Or during the fast of Ramadan, I still remember, the activity would become more aggressive. Early in the morning, three o'clock or four o'clock, I would see that the whole house was awake and there were people talking and praying. I would get up and they would say, "No, you sleep." And I would say, "No, I want to join you." And they would say, "You're too young to fast." But I used to insist, "I want to join you in the prayers and I want to make the fast."

EM: When do Muslim children begin to fast in Pakistan?

MZP: I used to do it myself when I was eight years old. It was not compulsory. The children are not discouraged at an early age. It varies from family to family. But when you are an adult, it becomes an obligation. When you're young, they encourage you and look after you but they don't make it very hard.

EM: What is your profession in the U.S.? What do you do here for a living?

MZP: I am a combustion and fuel engineer. In Pakistan I worked mostly on combustion projects. But I got interested in air pollution in Pakistan. Karachi is a city with a lot of smoke. I did an air pollution survey and took some measures to prevent air pollution. Then I decided to take some advanced studies in pollution. So first of all I wanted to come as a student to study.

At the time I was planning to go on for higher education, I was lucky because the Pakistani Council of Scientific and Industrial Research was planning to send me on for higher education. I was thinking of working in the U.S. I had heard there were a lot of problems here with air pollution. And so I applied for admission, and within three months my application was accepted. When I came to New York City I got a job with the New York State Department of Environmental Conservation in the air pollution program, because of my background in Karachi. They were doing a study in New York City, an air pollution monitoring program.

EM: In your everyday life as a professional and scientist, how is your identity as a Muslim expressed? Most of the people whom you work with know that you're a Muslim, right? At work do you have the opportunity to perform the prayers?

MZP: I have had no problem right from the start. I have very good staff to work with. I have very good superiors. They know me very well, and they have no objection. And I discussed this with them before I took the job. They told me, "You can do what you have to do, provided that it doesn't unnecessarily conflict with the work." And it never does because I perform *fajr*[2] and *maghrib*[3] at home and my night prayers too. At the coffee break, I do my *'asr*.[4] Fortunately, I worked at the World Trade Center and so I had no problem with *jum'ah*

---

[2]*Fajr* is the first of the five obligatory daily prayers for Muslims. It is performed before the rising of the sun.

[3] *Maghrib* is the prayer performed at sunset.

[4]*'Asr* is one of the five obligatory daily prayers. It is performed in the afternoon.

because I was three blocks from a *jum'ah* congregation. So I was very lucky.

EM: Are there any other Muslims in the area where you work?

MZP: Oh, yes. On Wall Street there is the Pakistani Bank, Arab businesses and stores, and things like that. There's no problem with the Friday prayers.

EM: How is your being a Muslim affected by living in North America? How would life as a Muslim here be different from Karachi?

MZP: I don't see any difference, except that people are Muslim in Karachi and you see the activities of prayer. But in normal life I don't see any difference. Here I have freedom to pray, as do most of the people in Karachi. I cannot speak for individuals. Nobody compels you in Pakistan. I can pray at home, I can pray at my work, and I can go to the mosque; there are mosques here also. I believe it would have been a different story if there were no mosques, if it were like in the Soviet Union where you can't go to the mosque; you are scared. There's freedom here.

There is one fundamental difference that I want to make very clear: the temptation from alcohol, which is forbidden, is much greater here. It's freer here. You are more exposed to those things that are forbidden and that you're to keep away from, you know, the music, the drugs, the fashions of the girls, mini skirts. You see people kissing and hugging each other in the trains.

EM: That would be different in Pakistan?

MZP: You keep away from those things and don't become mixed up with that part of the society. Especially for the younger generation the questions come up.

EM: Do you still work in the World Trade Center?

MZP: No, my office is in Queens.

EM: Is there a mosque nearby?

MZP: Oh, yes.

EM: Is there one near your home?

MZP: Yes, about five miles away.

EM: Are there large communities of Muslims there?

MZP: Yes. Where I live, there are not many. But where the mosque is there are quite a few. The mosque is in Flushing, Queens.

EM: Is there any one ethnic group that is predominant?

MZP: No. It's mixed.

EM: And your children, how old are they?

MZP: My oldest is twenty-two, another is twenty-one. There's one eighteen and the youngest is fifteen.

EM: How do you feel you're perceived as a Muslim by non-Muslims whom you know professionally or socially?

MZP: It depends, you see, on lifestyle. The way I dress, I look like everyone else. If I wore one of those long dresses or a head dress, then I would be different. When I go into the field to inspect industries, power houses, and they see my name, I can see a reaction on their faces. This is due to the Iranian situation. It is natural. But I have an excellent relationship with the people with whom I work. You have some sense of how you're perceived by others. As a Muslim it's your responsibility to be the best in your talk, your behavior and your attitude. I don't look down on people. There's a mutual respect. And by the way, they trust me more than anyone else in terms of honesty and time.

EM: Do you find any North American stereotypes towards Muslims, either that you have had to deal with personally or that you experience secondhand?

MZP: Most people see Islam in the cultural form first. They don't consider your attitude towards others and your behavior. They think that if you adopt the dress of Arabia, have a beard, put a *kaffiyeh*[5] on and have a long dress, that this is the fundamental. But it is not. It is your character that is fundamental in Islam. You are not a kind of actor who gets dressed up. You have to be real in your dealing with people. If I'm dirty and abusive and I say I don't care because I'm a Muslim and that's the way I live.... It's my behavior that's fundamental.

Sometimes you see Muslims using the *miswak*[6] on the street or spitting on the floor. They should realize that

[5]The *kaffiyeh* is a traditional head covering, which developed first for the practical reasons of protection from sun and sand rather than for religious reasons.

[6]The *miswak* is a type of toothbrush and toothpick used by Muslims.

there are other people watching who don't understand and may form an unfavorable opinion. The Prophet Muhammad (PBUH)[7] used the *miswak* because he was in Medina. Everybody else was doing it. There was a tradition and so people never objected. But here you use it in your bathroom, not openly.

People see some behavior practiced by Muslims who come here and behave differently. And they think this is Islam, but it is a stereotype. For example, in the subways you see people who say they are Muslims wearing white dresses. And they are projecting this behavior that has nothing to do with Islamic values. As a Muslim you can wear any type of dress you want, provided it is not immodest. The Prophet Muhammad (PBUH) lived in Medina, where there was a hot climate, so he adjusted himself to the tradition, the dress and the climate of that part of the world. But that culture cannot be imposed on an American culture and an American culture cannot be imposed on Africa, and African culture cannot be imposed on Southeast Asia. It is your behavior that counts.

EM: Have you found that non-Muslim Americans have an image of Islam that is not accurate?

MZP: Yes, I have experienced this — especially when I go to meetings and travel around. I have found that people have a very wrong perception of Islam. And when I talk to them, they say, "Is it really so?" Like terrorism, having four wives, women having no status. Things like this.

EM: Do you find this widespread?

-----

[7]See note, p. 6.

MZP: Oh, yes. People talk about thieves' hands being cut off, flogging, things like this. I'm not saying that these practices are not a punishment or a deterrent. How they are understood depends on the society. In New York City, people get robbed, burglarized, terrorized. And why? Because those who commit these crimes know there is no punishment. So they continue doing so. And in New York City, I don't think there's any reason for stealing or burglary, because there are so many programs for development and education, for help, for food stamps. Everything is available.

Islam says that it is the responsibility of the Muslim state to provide relief for the poor. During the time of Khalif Umar ibn Khattab,[8] a man was condemned to lose his hand. He protested. The verdict had been given and the judgment came to Umar. And Umar said that he wanted to talk to the man. The man said, "Umar, if your children had been starving, you would have done the same thing." Then Umar realized his responsibility and said, "It is my fault, not his fault." Then he suspended the judgment.

So this deterrent of cutting off the hand is only for people who have other means of help available. And if people are stealing, the ruler must be aware that there is something wrong. So there is a check and balance of rights and duties. But these teachings are misinterpreted, and people say, "Oh, my God! A hand cut off! What kind of an uncivilized society is this!"

I have talked with various people about the provision concerning four wives. I would like to explain this. In chapter 4 of the Qur'an, you can see that the problem came up with widows and orphans at that particular

---

[8] A khalif was the secular and religious head of a Muslim state. Khalif Umar ibn Khattab, the second khalif, died in 644 C.E.

time. That was the particular context. A woman should not have to live alone. And the same is true especially for the orphans.[9]

EM: What do you see as burning issues for Muslims in the U.S. and Canada and for Muslims throughout the world?

MZP: Because of the Iran situation the media have focused on the dark, negative Islam. That has created a lot of problems for the Muslims, especially our young children. The media do not give Muslims here the opportunity to reply. The campaign against Muslims is very aggressive. Our children ask why they should suffer for the acts of another country. It is politics; why should religion come into it? That campaign is something Muslims have every right to oppose. So we are trying to approach the Senate and Congress and to invite senators and representatives as well as media people to our banquets. And many flatly refuse because of politics. They say that if they go to a Muslim gathering "my constituency may not re-elect me." So we're not getting our message across.

EM: Do you think they fear that their constituency holds that Muslims are terrorists?

---

[9]In the Qur'an iv:3 it reads: "And if you fear that you cannot act equitably towards orphans, then marry such women as seem good to you, two and three and four; but if you fear that you will not do justice [between them], then [marry] only one or what your right hands possess [slaves]; this is more proper, that you may not deviate from the right course." Some modern Muslims hold that polygamy was permitted because of the emergency situation in which many men were being killed in battle and many children were being orphaned. Some Muslims hold that the limitation "but if you fear..." makes polygamy a practical impossibility.

MZP: Yes, they know that if they go to Muslim affairs their opponents can exploit it.

EM: Is your family Sunni or Shi'i?[10]

MZP: We are Sunnis. I don't call myself Sunni. I call myself Muslim.[11] I have no right to call myself Sunni, because the Qur'an says, "Don't divide yourselves into sects." If I say that I am Sunni or Shi'ite, I'm going against the Holy Qur'an. So we should call ourselves Muslims.

EM: What are other issues that you find important for Muslims?

MZP: The values of America are basically the values of the Qur'an. One nation under one God. It is one people and one Lord. Muslims are not aliens in American society.

EM: Are there any special concerns of Muslim youth today? What is important for your children?

MZP: It depends on how you bring them up. My children saw me praying, saw me very active in the mosque.

EM: Where do they go to school?

MZP: Public school. But they have seen me going to the Islamic Center every Sunday. And they go to the

[10]See note, p. 5.

[11]*Muslim* is a transliteration of an Arabic word that means "one who submits to God, who is wholly committed to the divine power and authority."

Islamic Center every Sunday and on holidays. They're totally involved and they receive personal guidance and join in discussion. In this society I cannot enforce anything on them. I can only tell them what is right and wrong. "This is the fire; if you put your hand in it, you get burned. You can either believe me or you can try it out. There are two ways. But some people don't listen; they want to try things for themselves. So there's an easy way to learn and a difficult way to learn. It's entirely up to you."

Thank God, my oldest son is twenty-two now and lives at home. He's in third year college studying to be a doctor. He's exposed to everything that goes on at school. His friends kid him about still living at home. But he laughs at them. He says that these people don't understand the values of life. They think that when you're eighteen you should get out of the home, you're an adult. I'm not claiming that we're a model. But my son says that he will get married and set up a home. He wants to marry a Muslim girl from Pakistan. They have seen me as an example. I have never forced anything.

EM: What do you wish Americans understood about Islam through you and through this book?

MZP: I think the first thing is education. We should not believe things through hearsay. We should learn from the source and see if something that has been said is correct or not. For example, I have studied Christianity and Judaism. And I have a better perception of Christianity and Judaism. I don't depend upon what anyone tells me. I went myself to the holy books. And then I formed my own opinion. And I judge it on the basis of the Holy Qur'an. In Islam the Holy Qur'an is very important. And I think those Christians who want to

study about Islam should get Islamic books, especially
the Holy Qur'an.

Islam is a total way of life. We are all human beings
who have been created by the one God. And we are
here on earth for a period. We are tried here. Good
deeds and bad deeds. And we will go back again to the
same God. So I would want people to know that Islam
is submission to the will of God. We have come from
God and we will go back to God. It is as simple as that.
We get guidance for what we must do and what we must
not do from the Holy Qur'an. So when I stand before
God I can say this is the book I practiced and this is the
model I followed.

3

Patricia Awad

Mrs. Awad, a native of Minnesota, is a convert to Islam. Mother of three grown children, she is a friendly, unassuming person and in a sense representative of the "average American." Mrs. Awad is active in the Islamic Center of Los Angeles. In addition to her work with her family and the Islamic Center, Mrs. Awad has been active in interfaith work in the Los Angeles area and has often been invited to lecture on Islam to students and school children there.

Patricia Awad: I'm from the Midwest, from Minnesota. And my parents are English, Norwegian and German. I'm a homemaker. I did secretarial work for a long time, but when it came to having my family and raising them, I felt my place was in the home. We did some economic figuring and figured it was just as feasible for me to stay home and take care of the family. And so I am a homemaker.

Elias Mallon: How many children do you have?

PA: We have three sons.

EM: And their ages?

PA: Unfortunately, they got old. I have not. The oldest lad is thirty-two; the middle one will be thirty; and the youngest is almost twenty-nine.

EM: What is your educational background?

PA: I finished high school in Minnesota and then came out here to California in the mid-fifties and met a very charming young man from the Middle East. We became emotionally involved and decided to get married. On New Year's Eve we will have been married thirty-four years. My husband, 'Abad, is from a little village near Jerusalem. It's a very small village named Kufr 'Aqab; it's right next to Ramallah.

EM: I was just over there recently, and the situation is very difficult. So your husband is Palestinian.

PA: Right.

EM: Tell me a little more about your family, your children. Are they Muslims too?

PA: Yes. All three of my sons are Muslims. We feel very strongly that this is an individual decision. They were raised as Muslims. But I'm proud to say that as they reached an age of reason and thinking, they decided that this was, in fact, the path they wished to walk. As they reached their high school years, we were not totally satisfied with the school system. So we enrolled them in a Catholic high school. I think that's part of where I got involved in the ecumenical movement myself.

Our sons did very well in school. They took religion as part of their curriculum and we made it a policy that when they came home from school we would simply discuss what they had studied that day and show how we would tell the story in Islam. As you probably know by now, there are a lot of parallels between Christianity and Islam, and there really isn't that much of a conflict in carrying on these stories. They're very fine young men. They're highly educated. The oldest boy has a Ph.D. in psychology; the middle one is an M.D., doing his residency in pediatrics; and the third is a lawyer, working for a rather prominent firm in the Los Angeles area.

EM: Can you describe something of your spiritual journey to Islam?

PA: First of all I had to make sure that this was, in fact, my path and not just due to my emotional involvement with my husband. He is a good man. He is a very spiritual man and feels his religion very strongly. But I had started studying comparative religion while I was in high school. And as I studied I really hadn't made up my mind quite where I belonged but I knew I was still searching, and I knew I am a religious person. I feel that God is very important in my life.

But the more I read, the more I felt that Islam seemed to be drawing me. So I mentally separated myself from my husband and did, in fact, make this decision about thirty years ago. I was not asked to; I was not forced to. There was no compulsion in this at all. My husband has never asked me to be a Muslim. I must confess that the day I made the decision and made my declaration was a great day because I really felt that 'Abad and I were walking the same path intellectually and spiritually as well as physically. And that's a good feeling in a marriage.

EM: In your everyday life today how you express your identity as a Muslim?

PA: Well, if you do any research into Islam at all you'll find that for people who are involved — truly involved — with their religion, it permeates every aspect of their life. It's not something you do occasionally. I am active in teaching about Islam to non-Muslims. And one of the first things that we point out is that people should not confuse the three monotheistic religions with their followers. Do not confuse Judaism with Jews or Islam with Muslims.

In this particular house we do not do anything without asking God's blessings on it. We are aware of His presence with us at all times. We fast; we do not drink any alcohol; we observe the rules of our religion as closely as we can, and try to be guided by the spirit of Islam — to take care of our fellow human beings and to live life in moderation.

EM: How is this affected by society? Is it helped, hindered, neutral?

PA: That's an interesting question, because as Muslims we have the responsibility to be out in society, not to ide from it or run from it. We must deal with it. And this is a strange society today. There's a serious lack of morals, a lot of amorality around. And so we have to look and make decisions for ourselves. We deal with everything on a step-by-step basis. One thing I tried to do as the boys were growing up. We're aware that there's a gutter out there but we don't bring it into the home. We respect our home; we respect the elders. We are a large, extended family; we believe in this very strongly. We believe in the effect an extended family can have on new, young members as they grow from infancy to old age. And so the society is out there, but we try to deal with it, not run from it.

EM: How and where do you worship?

PA: We have been very involved with the Islamic Center. Worship is strictly a one-to-one relationship with your Creator. As Muslims we build our faith on five pillars, one of which is prayer five times a day. And we observe these prayers. My husband is far more faithful in this than I. But then each goes at his own rate and own pace. We observe the dietary laws and we really try to follow the five pillars. We really do.

EM: How easy or difficult is it, for example, to find *halal* meat[1] in, say, the Los Angeles area?

PA: Well, there are several markets where you can purchase *halal* meat. But there have been statements

---

[1]*Halal* meat has been slaughtered and prepared according to Muslim standards and is, therefore, permitted to be eaten. Muslims do not eat pork and pork products, nor are they permitted to consume alcohol.

from the leadership at al-Azhar[2] that food that has been
killed in the name of God is permissible. And I prepare
the food, in the name of God. While I cook I recite the
bismillahirrahmanirrahim[3] and dedicate the food to God.
And therefore it becomes *halal*.

EM: Are you active at the Center? In terms of worship? For example, *jum'ah*.[4]

PA: Yes, we go to the Friday Prayers and the *'Id*
Prayers.[5] I taught at the Center for eight or nine years.
I'm semi-retired now because of a case of burn-out, I
guess you would say. But I am still involved. I'm going
out next Tuesday to give a talk at Cal State. I still speak
to high schools and once in a while teach a class at the
Center. But we're not as active as we were at one time.

EM: How do people respond to you as a Muslim? For
example, when you go to a church or a high school or
to Cal State to give a talk?

PA: I have never had anything but a very courteous
and respectful reception. I think they're a little surprised
because I am not what they envision; I am not an Arab.
I'm just a little old lady from the Midwest. And I think
it's a little bit of a surprise. I think they would be less
surprised if I were a younger person, because among
the younger generation there has been a lot of flowing

---

[2]Al-Azhar, an Islamic university in Cairo, Egypt, is one of the
oldest universities in the world.

[3]Literally, "In the name of God, the Compassionate, the Merciful."

[4]See note, p. 15.

[5]The special prayers of *'Id al-fitr* the celebration of the ending of
the fast of Ramadan.

between religions and ideologies. After the initial impact it's very workable.

EM: Are there any North American stereotypes about Muslims that you have had to deal with?

PA: Yes, yes, no doubt about it. You see the films, the movies, the media, all of the coverage. Everybody expects an Arab and a dagger and multiple wives behind them. What the cinema has done for the Muslim world is a great disservice. Muslims are people trying to live life and raise their children and survive and be self-sufficient, and there's really no big difference between Muslims and others.

EM: Have you had to deal with those stereotypes?

PA: Not too often. I think that maybe fifteen years ago there was a certain resentment toward anyone speaking about religion. And I think you would have found that in the Christian world as well as in the Muslim world. In the last few years there has been an openness to people involved with religion, and now there is more of an openness toward Muslims. I really feel that the world is growing smaller every day. And there is more awareness and more interest in learning about this. I was even asked to speak to a Kiwanis group. One man — a rabbi — came up to me and said, "We've never had anybody speak on religion before. Why now?" And he was told that because Islam figures very largely in the news today that it seemed important to their group to have some information to deal with. I'm finding that this is the reaction now. It's on an informational basis and that's how I deal with it.

EM: What do you see as burning issues for Muslims in North America and around the world?

PA: Well, we have a political situation that I don't choose to go into at all. That's not my field of expertise. I think the burning issue for any human being today is to have a relationship with their Creator in order to live and be a more moral human person. We are killing people right and left. We have complete lack of regard for the value of a human life. I think this is a burning issue to Muslims.

I think there is a lack of morality with regard to sexual freedom. My religion gives me tremendous freedom as a woman. I have every opportunity to do anything I want as a woman. But this does not mean an allowance for promiscuity or throwing away the values of a home or my self-respect as a woman. And I think these are burning issues. Not just for Muslims, but for all people.

EM: Having raised some children, what do you think are the concerns facing Muslim youths in America, for example, in the public education system and in a mass-media, consumer culture?

PA: The leaders lack information about Islam. The people who put out our textbooks, the people who select the curriculums for our schools, our political leaders have a very minimal knowledge of our religion. As an example: we put our boys in a Catholic high school. The first year the oldest boy was there they had a speaker from Egypt, a Christian, speak on Islam. And he gave some very bad misinformation. And of course the students immediately approached my son afterwards and said, "Is it true? Is this in fact part of Islam?" And he said, "Well, not actually; not quite the way it came out."

By the time my second son was in the school, they asked somebody from our Center to come and address them on the issue of Islam. And by the time the third one was there, the class went over to the Islamic Center. So once they were made aware that there was a a place to get the information, they utilized it. I think this is what's going on today. Our Muslim children want to fast and so they're different. Other kids don't fast for thirty days out of the year. Once there is education and information made accessible to the young people, they go along with it pretty well.

EM: Would your sons' experiences have been significantly different had they gone to one of the local public schools?

PA: I really don't think it would have been that different. I guess in Catholic school they did have to study re ligion every day. It was a smaller school, which was the main reason we made the transition. The public school was just too large. They were good students and they were being lost in the shuffle. As far as the religion, I don't think there would have been that much difference — public or private school, large or small. You're either going to try to follow your religion or you're not. And again this is the case of living in the society and dealing with it. But our transition from public to private was strictly because of numbers and the attempt to get a better quality education for the boys.

EM: What do you wish North Americans understood about Islam? What do you hope that your non-Muslim friends and colleagues understand about Islam, specifically from knowing you?

PA: There are several aspects of Islam that I think Americans just simply do not understand because of the textbooks that have been dealt them over the years. One, Islam is not spread by the sword. There is no compulsion in Islam. Women are not subservient in Islam. This is not a male-dominated religion. And we are normal people. I also think it's very important for the world as a whole to understand that not all Arabs are Muslims and, therefore, any political problems that exist affect Muslims and Christians and Jews. Not just Arab Muslims. Not all Arabs are Muslims and not all Muslims are Arabs. We have friends at the Islamic Center who come from just about every country in the world. From China, Pakistan, India, North America, from all over the Arab world, from England, Yugoslavia, you name it, we have people at the Center from everywhere. Islam is so universal. And it can work. All I have done in these last few years by going out and talking to groups is to try to inform, so that we can better accommodate each other with respect and affection.

EM: What are the groups that you have spoken to over the years?

PA: I've spoken mostly to high school students. Part of the speaking is related to the ecumenical dialogue with the Los Angeles archdiocese. I have also spoken to many comparative religion groups at the smaller universities and colleges that would bring groups to the Center. We've also had dialogue with several of the temples in the city, with the Stephen Wise Temple and Wilshire Boulevard Temple. This was Rabbi Magnam's organization, before he passed away.

I get a fabulous reaction from the young people. It is so interesting to see them interacting and asking questions. As long as the questions are asked with a sincere desire to learn there's no insult.

EM: Have you ever had unpleasant situations?

PA: No, I have had a couple of awkward situations with some of the teachers trying to corral the children. And I don't want that. I want the kids to be spontaneous and to really ask because that's how you learn. It's a little difficult to turn the teacher back and say, "Hold it. I can handle this. I'm not offended and I'm not hurt. It's quite workable and we can deal with it."

EM: If you could make any wish about the effect of a book like this, what would it be?

PA: Better understanding. Better understanding. I debated whether I should bring this issue up but I'm going to mention it to you. Recently you may have read or heard in the news about the man in the upper Midwest who had been sending hate mail. Well, I received one of these letters, unfortunately. I had gone back to Minnesota for my father's funeral. The day we came back from the cemetery I received a letter in the mail showing all sorts of clippings that said God does not believe in marriage between the races, that not even dogs marry between races. He said that we were condemned to hell, that we were defiling God's word. It was one of the most vicious things I have ever received. And this at a time when I was very vulnerable because of a death. It was very painful. I have three kids with high degrees. The youngest one finished his Bachelor's and Master's degrees simultaneously in four years. He is not a dog. He is a man with a mind. I was so offended and so hurt.

After I left Minnesota I threw the letter away because I didn't want my mother to see it. It seems various other members of my family received the same letter. We found out just this last year — some two and a half years later — that this man was finally tracked down through the Post Office. He had sent out well over a hundred thousand of these letters, including one to the head of one of the colleges in Minnesota who had adopted a Korean child. And those who knew this man said that he was such a gentle person; he had donated over $500,000 to build a new wing on a university there. And the school was going to keep the money but they were going to take his name off the building. They said that he was a very gentle man and they felt so sorry for him. But he genuinely felt he was doing the right thing. I don't think he was doing the right thing. And I find it very difficult in my heart to forgive and to forget. I'm not going to go out and try to destroy him; he's destroying himself.

This man could survive in this society today and feel that he was doing the right thing and have other people say, "Well he was a gentle soul!" That cannot undo the damage he has done to so many people. And if this type of mentality can still exist in this world today, then we have a problem.

I'm hoping this book will address that problem. We have to educate people. We are a nice, normal family. We hurt no one. We have educated our sons so that they will be proud of their Arabic background; they will be proud of their American background; they will be involved in their religious philosophy; they will contribute to society; they will be moral individuals and they pay taxes. What more could you ask for in this country? If we could educate people that that's all we're asking, then we will have achieved a great deal. One of the reasons I agreed to this interview is because I really feel it's important for

people to know how really dull and average we are —
just mainstream people.

EM: Have you experienced any Christian proselytiz-
ing towards you and your family?

PA: Yes, as a matter of fact, two or three times that are
rather outstanding. Once, a very dear friend of ours who
is interested in languages and has done a comparative
root study of Hebrew, Arabic, Greek and English was
coming to dinner with his wife. He called and asked if
they could bring a guest with them. We said, yes, of
course. Arab hospitality — the door was open. So they
brought the gentleman. We sat down at the dinner table
and he would not eat. As the story evolved it turned
out that he really felt that we were nice people but we
were condemned to hell because we were Muslim, so he
would not partake of our food. And we wondered, "Why
did you bother coming if you felt this way?" He did not
try to change our way of life; he did not give us a lecture
or a sermon that night. But he made it quite clear to
our friends that we were condemned to hell, and I really
could never figure our why he came. On other occasions
there were others as well who felt that we're nice people
but because we are Muslims we are condemned to hell.

Our friend, who brought this man to dinner, ultimately developed a brain tumor. And the night before
his surgery, he took my hand and asked me if I would
be with his wife during the surgery. He said, "I want
you here." And I said, yes, if you want me here I will
be here. As we left the hospital our friend's wife and
her other friends were there. And they asked me to stay
away the next day because they were afraid that, if he
were in a terminal situation, my presence there would
jeopardize his soul. And so the next day I waited. But

finally I said, " 'Abad, I'm sorry, I cannot break a promise to this man. I promised to be there and I have to go."

So we went to the hospital. I do not drive so my husband dropped me off. Just as I walked into the hospital the man's wife and her friend were walking toward me and the friend said, "Oh, we were just going to go to the chapel but you can't go there, can you?" And I said, "On the contrary, I've spent many hours in the chapel at Good Samaritan." When I'm distressed I can pray anyplace. I do not have to be in a mosque to pray. I pray in my own home. I can pray in a church. I can pray to God anyplace.

But we did not go to the chapel. We went up to the waiting room and just then they brought the man out of surgery. And the doctor came to his wife and said that it was a brain tumor, inoperable, malignant, and that there was a time limit for sure. And I remember his wife turned to me and took my hand. She didn't turn to her friend; she turned to me, took my hand, and said, "He really does believe in God, doesn't he?" And I said, "I don't know how you could ever doubt that. Of course he believes in God." He carries a copy of the Qur'an with him, but he's not declared as a Muslim. He just has such respect for this book.

He had chemotherapy for some time. My husband would drive him to these sessions. A year later we got a call. It was his birthday. We were supposed to go see him for his birthday, but his wife called and said, "Some other people will be there. Would you mind waiting for another few days and then come to visit?" Unfortunately, before we got there he passed away. And it was a sadness that these people had so little faith in God. They couldn't see that God could open the hearts of all people, not just certain types. It was a sad situation, but similar things have happened on other occasions.

EM: For example?

PA: That was the most dramatic case. We are, of course, inundated by Jehovah's Witnesses and Mormons coming to the door.

EM: But that isn't necessarily because you are Muslims.

PA: That's just door-to-door and the luck of the pick. I think the most fun is that when they become persistent, my husband says, "Come in. I have a message for you that I've been dying to share too." And they immediately leave and that's the end of that conversation.

4

Jimmy Jones

Jimmy E. Jones is a professor at Springfield College in Springfield, Massachusetts. In addition to his work at Springfield College, Professor Jones is a student at Hartford Theological Seminary and a volunteer chaplain in the Connecticut prison system. Mr. Jones brings a broad spectrum of interests and experience to this interview.

Elias Mallon: What are your ethnic and cultural origins?

Jimmy Jones: African-American.

EM: Where are you living here in North America?

JJ: New Haven, Connecticut.

EM: And your profession?

JJ: I'm a college administrator at Springfield College, School of Human Services.

EM: What is your educational background?

JJ: I have a Master of Arts in Religion from Yale Divinity School. I spent two years in Yale Law School. I have an undergraduate degree in secondary education from Hampton Institute. I'm presently at Hartford Seminary in a Doctor of Ministry program.

EM: Tell me a little about your family background. Were you a Muslim as a child?

JJ: No. I was born in Baltimore, Maryland, and I was raised in Roanoke, Virginia, by extended family — my cousins — and I was a very active member of the High Street Baptist Church in Roanoke. And the rest of the family was also active. I had five siblings, but they were living in Baltimore. I was the only child in the household in Roanoke. That was the family that I grew up in until I was eighteen years old. Then I went to college. Then I came to New Haven and went to law school. I've been in New Haven ever since — the past twenty years.

EM: Could you tell me something about your spiritual journey towards Islam?

JJ: My first recollection of knowing anything about Islam was when I was probably in the fourth or fifth grade in 1958 or '59. I was traveling with the Harrison

Elementary School boys choir. We went to Washington
and we went by a place where they sold bean pies. I remember seeing well-dressed men there and women with
their heads covered wearing white, long gowns. I never
heard anyone refer to them as Muslims. If they did, it
wasn't in my consciousness. That's my first recollection.

I think my most dramatic encounter had to do with
reading *The Autobiography of Malcolm X*. I was between
my sophomore and junior years at Hampton Institute.
Subsequent to reading *The Autobiography of Malcolm X*,
I went to the library to read everything I could about
Islam. And it became quite apparent to me, from reading and from visiting what were then the temples of the
Nation of Islam, that what was in the books really was
not the same thing that was being taught at the temple.
The books weren't by Muslims, they were by Western-
ers, orientalists. As a result of that and other reading, I
became more active in black power and civil rights.

When I came to New Haven in '68 I began attend-
ing the temple on a fairly regular basis. It got to be
once a week. I was not a member. I did not become
a member — take *shahadah*[1] — until October 1979, well
after the Nation of Islam had dropped its racist trappings
and become a more "orthodox" organization. I became
a member of the Masjid[2] Muhammad in New Haven at
that time. That's how I became a Muslim.

EM: I'm interested in the difficulties you might have
living as a Muslim in North America.

JJ: Well, with my daughter there have been problems

---

[1]*Shahadah* is the Muslim proclamation of faith that there is no god
but God and that Muhammad is the messenger of God. It is the act
that constitutes a person as a Muslim.

[2]Masjid is the Arabic word translated into English as "Mosque."

about dating. The biggest fight my eighteen-year-old and I have had was because I always wanted her chaperoned on her dates, usually by someone older, but my compromise was to allow her younger brother to accompany her. We're very close, and it was as if I didn't trust her, she said. How could I do this to her? She would sneak around — which she doesn't ordinarily do. That's just not the kind of person she is. I was cooking at the time and she made me spoil the meal. We really upset one another about this.

As a Muslim parent, particularly with my daughter, but even with my oldest son, I always ask, "Where are you going? Who are you going to be with? How long are you going to be there? Is alcohol going to be served? Are there parents going to be around? Is there a phone number I can call to reach you?" A lot of that came from Islam and some of it came from my Christian upbringing. It is a struggle because everybody else is going to parties with alcohol even as teenagers. Thirteen-, fourteen-, fifteen-year-old girls are going out on dates. It's very, very difficult.

EM: What do you wish North Americans understood about Islam? What do you wish that your non-Muslim friends and colleagues understood about your religion from knowing you?

JJ: I want North Americans to understand that the most important thing about a Muslim is his or her behavior. We're human beings just like the rest. We have the same wants and desires. We happen to believe that everybody is basically born Muslim and therefore everyone is born to serve God. We wish to live in peace with people, particularly other people who worship God. It's not our intention either to fight with or denigrate Christianity or Judaism or, for that matter, any other religion as long as those religions, those people, try not to infringe upon our religious freedom. And that's a basic tenet of America.

We really want to be a part of peoples' communities. Muslims are getting more active in politics, getting more active in developing their own businesses. We want people to know that we're not ogres and we're not trying to convert people to Islam. We believe, as many Christians believe, that only God converts people anyway. And so we're people of peace. I think my colleagues already know this about me. I mean there are things we don't like about what people do and how they do it, and we say so. But we still can work together.

EM: One of the things I hear from prison chaplains, most of whom are Christians, is that it is increasingly clear that since they are working in the prison system they are going to have to have a better understanding of Islam. This is because there are a lot of Muslims with whom they come in contact and others who will become Muslims. Since you work as a chaplain in a prison, I am personally curious about how successful Islam is with the prisoners. I suspect you work with men mostly. How successful is Islam in changing their lives when they get out of prison?

JJ: What do I think attracts prisoners to Islam? The largest percentage of the people I see in prison, seventy-five, eighty percent, are African-American. The Prophet Muhammad was an orphan. Even though in some ways his persecution wasn't as violent as other persecutions we've seen, nonetheless he was persecuted for his beliefs. He was ostracized. He left his homeland, in my view at God's bidding. He made a pilgrimage. I think

that for African-Americans there's a lot of identification
with that. We were taken from our homeland to a land
that is not ours. "How can you sing the Lord's song in
a strange land?" The discrimination that we feel makes
Islam attractive to us because it's a way of rejecting the
culture that will not have us. In sociological terms I think
that one of the reasons that many African-Americans go
to Islam as opposed to Christianity — and many of us
have been raised Christian — is that the people doing
these things to us are also Christians.

Another factor — and this is part of what attracted
me to Islam — is direction and discipline. I would ar-
gue that religion answers three fundamental questions:
where we came from; how we should act while we're
here; and where we're going. You could put everything
about a religion under these three points. I was very active in the church. I taught Sunday school, I wrote the
Christmas pageant, I was in the choir. But Islam is more
comprehensive for me; it makes creation more under-
standable to me. One problem in the Christianity I was
taught was that I understood the King James Version of
the Bible to be the way Jesus Christ spoke. There are
many people who live in America and still believe that.
I leave that at the door of humanity and not of God.

The point is that I was looking for something that
made more sense. As for direction and discipline, Islam demands that you be Muslim seven days a week,
twenty-four hours a day. The formal worship of God is
demanded of you every time the sun rises. You begin
with *fajr* prayer.[3] It is demanded of you whether you do
it or not. It is required of you to make your prayers five
times a day. *Zakat*[4] is required of you. It is not something

---

[3]See note, p. 17.
[4]See p. 10.

you can take or leave or that you want to do because it's extra. The fast during the month of Ramadan is required. *Hajj*,[5] if you have the wherewithal, is required. Bearing witness, however you interpret it, is required of a Muslim. That was attractive to me.

I think that one reason why Islam is attractive to a person in prison is that many of our youngsters end up in prison because they lack direction and discipline. There are some forms of Christianity that don't make these demands. Whereas most forms of Islam, even those that in our view aren't Islam, give direction and discipline. And that's what makes it attractive. And then you add the attraction of the black nationalist aspect of the Nation of Islam in a place where the majority of people are African-Americans. In a sense, the story of Islam in prisons is the story of Malcolm X, because the attraction for Malcolm X was a nationalist attraction. But ultimately he made the pilgrimage and his eyes were opened. A lot of youngsters join a group called the "Five Percenters," which is essentially little more than a street gang. Often, not always, they end up as what we could call orthodox Muslims. And it's a spiritual journey much like the spiritual journey for Christians.

EM: Have you been able to do any kind of follow-up on African-American prisoners who have become Muslims to determine what happens in their lives when they leave prison?

JJ: Not formally, but the Masjid al-Islam was started in New Haven at the urging and hard work of a couple of guys that I used to work with in prison.

---

[5]The *hajj* is the pilgrimage to Mecca, one of the pillars of Islam.

EM: So their lives were changed?

JJ: Oh, yes, for these two. I was downtown talking to one of them yesterday. He's working two jobs. He's been out three years now.

EM: Would you find then a fairly low rate of recidivism?

JJ: Among Muslims? No, because a large number of youngsters — seventeen, eighteen, nineteen years old — are attracted to the religion for the wrong reasons. There are two reasons. One, they want to be in a group. Two, it will make them look good in court. It's also unsettling to the administration, to parents, to everybody in authority. If they work through these reasons and if they study the religion, they're more likely to stay out of trouble. But often they're just enamored with the Arabic and feel like they're joining a secret society. I try to downplay that part of it.

I think what prepared me for being a Muslim was being raised in the Baptist church. I was learning the idea of the power and the sovereignty of the law when I sang the doxology even though it included the Trinitarian concept, which we don't care for. I see far too many guys who take the *shahadah* and then I see them six months later. The conversion is superficial. But I think that for a significant number, not a majority but a significant number, it's real.

5

Syed Manzoor Naqi Rizvi

Syed M. N. Rizvi is a cardiologist in New Jersey. He is involved in publishing The Message of Peace, *a magazine dedicated to spreading information about Islam. Among Shi'ite Muslims, the term "Syed" indicates that its bearer is descended from the family of the Prophet Muhammad. This is a title of honor, which to Western non-Muslims who are not acquainted with the practice sometimes appears to be a first name.*

Syed Manzoor Naqi Rizvi: My name is Manzoor Naqi Rizvi. Syed M. Rizvi is not my name. *Syed* comes from the Prophet's daughter, Sayedah, and Rizvi is the family name from my forefather, who was an Imam.[1]

Elias Mallon: Your family comes from India?

SMNR: Yes, we are originally from Bihar. That's in the central part of India. In 1926 my father migrated to Uttar Pradesh, in the northern region, where we have lived since. According to our family tree, which is contained in a large book of about two hundred pages, we Rizvis take our origin from the eighth Imam, the descendant of the Prophet Muhammad. His name was Imam Ali al-Rida. And from Rida it became Rizvi. Our forefathers emigrated from Iran to India and settled in Bihar. All the names of forefathers back to Imam Rida are contained in that book, which now also includes the names of my children. It's a large book and everything is there.

EM: Bihar is a state in India?

SMNR: Bihar is one state and Uttar Pradesh is another state. My father migrated from Bihar to Uttar Pradesh, from a small town to a larger town. We were all completely educated in Lucknow, which is a very big town.

EM: Was the cultural setting of your town Muslim? Shi'a? Or was it Hindu?

SMNR: No, it is a mixed population. Uttar Pradesh is about fifteen to twenty percent Muslim, and the rest are non-Muslims.

EM: Are most of the Muslims there Shi'ite?

---

[1]See note, p. 9.

SMNR: No. Only twenty or thirty percent are Shi'a. The rest of them are Sunnis.[2]

EM: How long have you lived here in the United States?

SMNR: Since 1973. In India I finished my Bachelor's degree. I did an M.B.B.S., which is equal to an M.D. here, and then I did one year training. I spent a couple of years in Saudi Arabia. And then I had a five-year training period here, which completed my training.

EM: Tell me a little about your family here in the United States.

SMNR: My younger brother, an engineer, came first in 1971. Then he called me. I wasn't really interested at that time in coming here. Then he pressed me and I came here from Saudi Arabia. I also have cousins here. Then there's my wife and I, and we have four children.

EM: How old are your children?

SMNR: My oldest son is eighteen, my daughter is sixteen, and the two younger boys are eight and two.
While we are talking about family background, let me tell you about my father. All my relatives were left in Bihar, or, after Pakistan was formed, they migrated to Pakistan. So we in Uttar Pradesh were a small family. My father is a very learned person. He did not master English but he did have mastery of Arabic, Persian and Urdu. He is highly qualified in religious jurisprudence and religious sciences. He was a school teacher and is

[2]See note, p. 5.

very highly respected for his social and community services, his high moral character and his religious knowledge. He is well-known all over India and Pakistan for
his knowledge and his progressive nature in religious
matters. He is famous among the *'ulema* as the most
progressive *'alim*.[3] For example, he encouraged people
to send their daughters as well as their sons to school.
He is a religious teacher and a speaker and a good writer.
His two brothers were also religious scholars.

My father is a very charismatic person who is loved
by non-Muslims as well as Muslims. He would go out of
his way to help anyone regardless of caste, creed, age or
sex. Although he taught us to read, we learned mainly
from his character. Because of his progressive ideas, we
eight brothers and two sisters could get higher education
in our respective fields.

Religion was all around us. My father had a large
religious library. He used to be invited from place to
place to give lectures on Islam. But at the same time he
was a very practical man. He used to write for many
magazines. That is the way that we learned — in the
home, through the practice of the religion itself.

EM: In your everyday life today, how do you express
your identity as a Muslim?

SMNR: That is an interesting question. One of our
Imams, Imam Ja'afar as-Saddiq, the sixth Imam, said that
if you want to judge a person, don't judge him when he's
praying or when he's fasting. Judge him in his day-to-
day actions of life: when he's walking, when he sees a
person who has fallen, whether he goes out of his way

---

[3] *'Ulema* is the plural of *'alim*, which means a learned person.
The *'ulema* correspond, though not exactly, to official teachers and
theologians.

and helps him. That's how you judge a person in a real
sense. For us Islam is a way of life; we practice it all
the time. For example, if I go to see a patient, it's in my
mind that this is not only my career, but a moral and
religious obligation. My Creator is watching me. We are
Muslims and we have to be a little bit more courteous to
the patient. We are always mindful of questions and our
answers on the Day of Judgment. The bedside manner
probably means a little bit more to us than to others. I'm
not saying that we have the best manners in the world,
but they are supposed to be the best. If I am alone or if
I am with other people I will try my best to behave well,
respectfully, because we believe that God is watching us,
and we are answerable to Him.

EM: How is your being a Muslim and specifically a
Shi'ite affected by the fact that you live in North America, the United States?

SMNR: In one sense, not at all. I am as much or
probably more a practicing Muslim than I was before.
On the professional side, my colleagues and my pa-
tients do not seem to be bothered in general. It is true
that most professional people from places other than the
United States know more about Muslims than Americans
do. For example, there are doctors from South America, south India, Ceylon, the Philippines. Most of them
know something about Muslims. But most U.S. professional people, because they are so busy, don't have the
time to learn about Muslims, even if they wanted to.
When they see that someone is a Muslim and a Shi'ite,
they are startled a bit. But usually there's no big problem, and besides, most of our contact is during business
hours.
Once in awhile, sometimes in social life, it may pose

some questions. Going into people's homes can be a little problem because for some, beer is like a cup of tea is to us. But when they offer it to us, we don't drink. Most understand this, but sometimes someone will say, "Well, a little bit doesn't matter." Once at dinner, someone asked, "How can you eat beef but not pork; meat is meat." I'm not blaming them; but they don't realize. It is not really an obstacle to a good friendship. Definitely not.

EM: It's a lack of sensitivities in some people, or lack of understanding?

SMNR: I think both. Nobody has time to understand each other. And lack of understanding develops insensitivity. On a one-to-one basis, Americans in general are nice, tolerant people. But sometimes they don't understand Islamic activities or customs, because they have not lived with them. I'll give you an example. When a representative from a pharmaceutical company comes into my office, the nurse may mention that I am fasting. The representative asks about my fasting. "So you're a Muslim?" "Yes." "So you can marry four girls." Then I say, "Sit down. You tell me about your product and I'll tell you about my product." Islam is not only four marriages.

EM: Do you get a chance to worship with other Muslims, other Shi'a?

SMNR: Oh, yes.

EM: What is the Shi'i community like here? How

many people are part of it? Are they be mostly from the
subcontinent?[4]

SMNR: We have a big community in the metropolitan area that extends from Connecticut to Philadelphia.
We should have about ten thousand people. And we
communicate very well. Muharram[5] is an important
month for us.

EM: And Ashurah?[6]

SMNR: Right, which goes for ten days. But it usually goes for two months, remembering Imam Hussein.
And Muharram is the month that we see almost everyone. People come from north New Jersey and south New
Jersey and all over. We have a few meeting places.

EM: Do you mean a Shi'i center?

SMNR: Yes, religious centers.

EM: Do you have a mosque here in New Jersey?

SMNR: We have a mosque here in Englewood and a
place in south New Jersey.

EM: How many people frequent them?

---

[4]The subcontinent of Asia: India and Pakistan

[5]Muharram is the first month of the Muslim lunar calendar. On the
tenth of Muharram, the Shi'a observe the anniversary of the death of
Imam Hussein b. 'Ali b. Talib, the younger grandson of Muhammad.

[6]Although 'ashurah is a word used by both Sunni and Shi'i Muslims, the meaning that each group has for this term is quite different.
For Shi'a, 'ashurah, the tenth day of the month of Muharram, is the
anniversary of the death of Imam Hussein.

SMNR: That depends. On a very important day there would be five hundred people or even more.

EM: Are there any other activities related to it, like a school?

SMNR: There is a Sunday school. There's a Thursday evening gathering to recite *du'a*.[7] Then we have a brief lecture and *tafsir al-Qur'an*.[8] The next day, on Friday, we have the Friday prayer, and then on Sunday we have the school.

EM: Is that school for children or adults?

SMNR: Adolescents and children. Adults come for *tafsir al-Qur'an*. Also we have an Islamic Center directorate with a director from Pakistan and a secretary. It is in Englewood. The adult school in central New Jersey.

EM: Have you had to deal with any other North American stereotypes about Muslims? You've mentioned the stereotype about four wives. Are there others?

SMNR: Yes, there are. Many Americans think "All Muslims are terrorists." Or they think of poor, uncivilized, old-fashioned people. Sometimes people think that all Muslims are Arabs and all Arabs are Muslims.
The media has presented us like some undesirable creatures. Especially when talking of the Shi'a, forget it — they talk about us as hard-core difficult people. In general, if you meet people face to face, they end up appreciating you. But in the background there is an air

---

[7]Non-obligatory prayer; supplications.
[8]*Tafsir al-Qur'an*, literally "interpretation of the Qur'an," is the religious science of explaining the meaning of the Qur'an.

of mistrust and misconceptions. There are two main reasons for this: the local people's lack of knowledge and the anti-Muslim, anti-Islamic propaganda in the media. This mistrust of course is not common in physician-physician or physician-patient relations, but it is in the air and you can smell it distinctly.

EM: Have your children had any trouble in school?

SMNR: Yes. For example, for a long time my daughter didn't declare her identity as a Muslim. Because in spite of knowing that my daughter is a Muslim, the teachers would talk a lot of garbage about Islam in the class.

EM: Does your daughter go to public school?

SMNR: No, she goes to a private Catholic school. I keep writing to the school authorities hoping to talk with them about the literature they use to teach about religions. I have told them that my daughter cannot take a dance course. The teacher agreed. I also said that during sports hours she has to wear complete clothing; she cannot wear shorts. Again the teacher agreed.

EM: And your son?

SMNR: The eight-year-old is in second grade. He's also in Catholic school. As young as he is, I say to him, "Tell them you are Muslim." He says, "No, I can't do that." He is a little bit embarrassed. I can't pinpoint anything that my children have suffered in terms of grades or merits because of prejudice. I doubt very much that such has happened. But the textbooks are terrible. We

write letters of protest all the time, but so far, our protests
have fallen on deaf ears.

EM: What do you see as burning issues for Muslims
in the United States and Canada?

SMNR: Many problems for Muslims in the U.S. are
the same as for non-Muslims. The other day I heard a
priest in New York give a lecture about the deterioration
of morality in the U.S. In his inaugural address George
Bush talked about "a kinder, gentler America." We Muslims probably have the same problems as educated persons and religious persons in all the other communities:
the general deterioration of morality in the country. We
have too much materialism, and we have broken all the
bonds of ethics and morality.

EM: So Muslims face basically the same problems
that confront others?

SMNR: I'm sure that's true. But for Muslims the
problems become more acute, especially in relation to
their children.
The news on T.V., radio, in newspapers, all starts from
sex, drugs and murder, and ends in arrests, shoot-outs
or cop-killings. When I read, when I talk to people, it's
the same. Even the cartoons, as well as other T.V. programs, are full of violence and sexual deterioration. I
don't watch T.V. at all, but I have to let my son watch
cartoons, and all of them end up in something abnormal.
For our children these problems are more acute. At home
they have been given a different set of moral standards
about sex, abortion, drugs, respect for parents. At school
it's just the opposite. They see a different attitude there,
and have great peer pressure to do wrong. For example,

when my older son went into ninth grade, in the first lecture parents and children were both there. The point the speaker made is that now you young people are on your own. How old was my son? He must have been fourteen. "You're on your own. You do not have to listen to your parents." The speaker could probably have put it in a different way. I know he meant no harm, but the way he put it, some of the children may think that they are now liberated. That really bothers us.

Major problems at this time include the sexual problems in the schools, lack of understanding between fathers and mothers, divorce, the disregard for life, the terrorist label applied to Islam. These are common. There is general disregard for law and order. From top to bottom, every aspect of life has some problem from a moral point of view. Even people who are supposed to protect the law are taking bribes. Don't take me wrong. This is very common in India and other countries. We were very happy to come here for that reason.

EM: What do you wish that North Americans understood about Islam? What do you wish your non-Muslim friends and colleagues would learn about Islam from knowing you?

SMNR: First, they should understand us as normal human beings. We are no different from anybody else. And the religion that we follow is not an entirely different religion from Judaism and Christianity. A lot of things are very common to them. They should try to understand us more than they do and to understand that the religion of Islam can bring extremely beneficial things to this society.

We have a lot of regard for life, great regard for human life and even animal life. We are not supposed to harm any person, any living creature, without a good reason. We should also like to tell them that our religion, especially the Shi'ite, has a basic code in the sense that education, knowledge and common sense are very high on our agenda. Regard for life, education, and, of course, the oneness and justice of God are basic tenets, which we believe and practice. We would like people to know this.

The media can do a lot to spread these good tidings. They have spread a lot of confusion about us; it is high time that they give Americans some truth about Islam.

EM: Does your community have much contact with Sunni Muslims?

SMNR: Yes, we do. They come to our lectures. We have organized four lectures a year. In New York, New Jersey, different places. We have Imam Ali Day, Imam Hussein Day, Prophet Muhammad Day, Islam Day. And not only Sunnis come here but also Christians; Christian lecturers come for talks.

EM: Do you notice any difference in the relations between Sunnis and Shi'a in the United States and in India? Were there good relations between the two communities where you lived in India?

SMNR: Yes. We had very good relationships in the place where we lived in India. Of course, in some places there was misunderstanding, but in general the relations were very good, and this goes back centuries. When it comes to enumerate the differences, I can enumerate a hundred. But we have lived together all our lives without any big problem. We believe in one God, we believe in the same Prophet, we believe in the same Qur'an. The beliefs are the same. Of course, there are some groups who will fight for any reason. Among both Shi'a and Sunnis there are people like this.

EM: Generally you have found in the United States a relatively good relationship between the Shi'a and Sunnis?

SMNR: There is a good relationship, that is true. In India there were relations that went back a hundred years. There were intermarriages. But here we are creating the relationship. That is a difference. There are good relations; it is a very healthy relation. For people who understand, we don't even talk about it. Sunnis come to our parties — birthday parties, religious parties. They come all the time and we really enjoy each other. At the same time, we also have non-Muslims there. There has been a very smooth relation — except for those humps that are produced by splinter groups that take advantage of the difference.

6

Dawud Assad

Dawud Assad was born in Palestine and is a survivor of the Deir Yasin massacre. He has lived in Jordan and the United States. Mr. Assad was educated both abroad and in the United States and is a mechanical engineer. He is presently Associate Director of the World Muslim League and a member of the Council of Masajid (Mosques). Actively engaged in interfaith relations in the New York area, Mr. Assad has made a major contribution to understanding between Muslims and adherents of the other religions of the New York metropolitan area.

Dawud Assad: I came from a small village in Palestine called Deir Yasin. Deir Yasin is about two miles west

63

of Jerusalem. And there are about eight hundred people down there; everybody knows each other. I was actually born in Jerusalem and lived in Deir Yasin all my life until 1948, when a great massacre took place there on April 9.[1] In that massacre — probably everybody heard about it — I lost about thirty-eight people of my own, including my grandmother, who was ninety-six years of age. Her name was Hajjah Aminah. And my younger brother, 'Omar. He was two years of age and he was on her shoulders and he was killed. My sister was with them and they thought she was killed but — after my grandmother and brother were shot — she slipped in between them and fell asleep. Later on she was taken captive.

I was at that time about sixteen years of age and I managed to escape. When I saw my uncle behind me get shot — I was just going down the steps — I managed to be a little bit faster and I ran and I threw myself in a ditch. During the time of the Ottoman Empire,[2] it had been a fortification ditch. I threw myself there and I started to creep on my belly. And I remember at that time I had a lot of hair. When I'd come to a shallow place and my head showed up, I'd see the bullets go bzz, bzz, bzz over my head. And I'd see my hair going up,

---

[1] Deir Yasin was attacked by the Stern Gang, Zbai-Leumi and Hagganah, Israeli terrorist groups. During the attack several hundred civilians, men, women, and children, were killed.

[2] The Ottoman Empire, with its capital in Istanbul (formerly Constantinople) and ruled by the Sultan, governed Egypt, the Levant, Turkey, Greece and the Balkan peninsula. According to legend the Ottoman dynasty was founded by a tribal chieftain by the name of Ertoghrul. The empire took its name from Osman, the son of Ertoghrul, who died in 1326. The Sultan Mehmed II conquered Constantinople on May 29, 1453, bringing the thousand-year Byzantine Empire to an end. The Ottoman Empire came to an end with the exile of the last sultan, Mehmed VI, and the proclamation of the Turkish Republic by Mustafa Kemal (Atatürk) on October 29, 1932.

with the air coming over it. And then I went to the west side of the village because my house was exactly in the middle between our village, Deir Yasin, and the Jewish settlements, which were on the east side. So I had to run to the west side of the village, where the villagers were, so that I could escape. Where I was going — my own village — they thought that I was Jewish ... they were shooting at me. So I was between two fires. And then I managed to reach the village and from there I went to a nearby village, Ain Kerem, and was scared but. . . . It was a terrible massacre.

From there I went to Jerusalem because I wanted to see who was alive. You see, first we were attacked by the Stern and the Zbai Leumi — this terrorist organization — but later on they said that the Hagganah came. And the Hagganah also, they say, started to take captives. They put the captives in one house, and my mother and my sister were put in that house. And they took these captives and they put them in trucks and then they started to parade. Then they put them in the Jewish settlements, and then after that the Jewish leaders started to take the clothes off all the women, hoping that they would find some jewelry.

My mother and sister were missing, taken captive, and we understood that after they were searched they were taken to a house near a small hotel in Jerusalem. I went down to see if my mother and sister and also other relatives were alive. I saw my brother and my sister there and some of my relatives who had escaped. I had about thirty-eight people — cousins, uncles, aunts — who were killed.

There is a story about my sister, who managed to go to the house where the captives were in Deir Yasin. My mother, Nazha Attiyeh, asked Nazihah, my sister, "Where's your brother Dawud?" "Where's your Uncle

Adwan?" My uncle had been with me. She said, "Uncle Adwan was killed and I saw him in the house, and Dawud, I don't know, they probably killed him. I don't know where he is. But my grandmother and my brother 'Omar were killed over there. If you want, I'll show you where they were killed."

So my mother asked one of the officers from the Hagganah to let her go and see my grandmother and my brother. When she went there she saw my brother, 'Omar, who was two years of age at that time. She took him in her hand and she could not find any blood at all, but he seemed unconscious or dead. He was not moving. But my grandmother was all in blood. So we thought that probably when my grandmother was shot he fell on his head on a rock and just lost consciousness and passed away.

My mother asked the officer if she could take him with her. He said, "No, if you don't put him down here I will shoot you." So my mother had to leave him and up till now she doesn't know whether he really was . . . what happened to him. But he probably was. . . . In the meantime smoke was coming out of a nearby house. It was my Aunt Basmah's house. So my mother asked the officers, "Look, there's a grenade, a fire grenade over there in that house and the children are screaming. It's my relative's house. Let me go and take the kids."

He said, "No, don't go there because you will be killed." And she was still hearing the screams of the children in the fire. At that house about twelve people in my Aunt Basmah's family were killed. It was a terrible, terrible incident.

After that we went to Amman, Jordan. I finished my high school education in Hussein College in Amman. It was 1949 when I graduated. And then I went to Egypt, the American University at Cairo, for one year. I got a grant and aid from that university because I was a refugee from Palestine.

Then I decided to come to the United States. I arrived in September of 1951. I went to Rutgers University in New Brunswick. Then I finished my B.S. degree at Northeastern University. I'm a mechanical engineer.

Elias Mallon: How important was religion in your family when you were growing up?

DA: Well, my father and my mother always prayed at home. I can remember my father getting up early for the *fajr*, the dawn prayer.[3] I was very young at that time. It was so beautiful that it sticks in my mind.

When I grew up I repeated what my father always did. Later, when we went to Jordan as refugees, we lived by a mosque. In Amman, you hear the call of prayer five times a day. Especially the dawn prayer, *fajr*. You would first hear the Qur'an recitation and then *tasbih*,[4] the glorification, and then the prayer.

Being surrounded by the atmosphere there, being near the mosque, we used to go to almost all the prayers. When you're living in an Islamic atmosphere like this, all your family's affected and also all the neighbors. And besides, in our high school — the one I went to in Jordan — religion was an essential part of the curriculum. You had to pass the religion course before a degree was given to you. We used to have about three hours of religious instruction a week. It was a major part of school. We always studied about religion and listened to our elderly sheikhs and imams, and this affected me a lot.

EM: In terms of your life, your work and everything

---

[3] See note, p. 17.
[4] A Muslim exclamation proclaiming the glory of God.

else here in the United States, how is your identity as a
Muslim expressed?

DA: I started working at the Muslim World League
about ten years ago. But professionally I am a mechanical engineer. After I graduated in 1959 I worked in com-
panies like Kimberly Clark, Lipton Tea, and Servisco. I
was a chief engineer and was traveling a lot.

What impressed me there was this: when we'd go for
an evening business meeting, of course I always asked
what the food would be, because sometimes they would
have ham or bacon. So I would order beef.[5] So everybody would be eating ham, and then here I come with
the steak. And everyone would ask me, "How come
you have a steak and we all have ham?" So I told them
I was a Muslim. And I was really very proud of it. I
thought they would probably get uncomfortable. But I
found them very respectful. I was different and they
were asking about my religion. I explained it to them,
the discussion would go on and they would tell me, "We
respect you very much because of this" — because of the
way I behaved.

I try to be very polite with all people. I try to show
by my actions that I am a Muslim. I don't hate anybody.
I speak good with everybody. I speak about my religion.
One time when we were going on a trip to Ohio — there
were about seven of us — we asked the bus driver if he
could make a stop for us to make *'asr* prayer.[6] And he
was very nice. He stopped the bus; we made *'asr* prayer
and when we came back after a ten-minute break, people
on the bus asked us, "What were you doing?" We told
them we were Muslims and we have to say our prayers.

---

[5]See note, p. 6.
[6]See note, p. 17.

Actions like this make people ask about your religion. Then it's like you are a *da'i*, like a missionary. So I felt comfortable and I found that in this country, the USA, there is freedom of religion. We could meet, we could say anything we want. There are no restrictions and I like that very much, especially freedom of worship, freedom of speech. Unfortunately we are lacking these in our country.

EM: But generally you've found that people are receptive and respectful of you as a Muslim?

DA: Yes. Of course not all the people are. You find people here who don't like religion. For instance, because of the distortion of the image of Islam, when you say, "I am a Muslim," or "I'm an Arab," right away some people think that you are a camel driver, or you live in the desert, or you have a lot of harems. And they always accuse you of being a terrorist. I explain to them that this is not so, that there are good Christians and bad Christians, good Muslims and bad Muslims, good Jews and bad Jews. And you should not think that all Muslims are bad or all Christians are bad or all Jews are bad, because you cannot make a generalization. But the image, unfortunately, in this country is that Muslims are terrorists.

EM: So you would say that one stereotype of Muslims is that they are terrorists.

DA: Yes, and not only that. On T.V. you see the Arabs as the bad guys. Either thieves or killers or people like that.

EM: Are you able to worship, go to Friday prayer, with other Muslims? And in what kind of a setting?

DA: Well, most of the people who are working in America unfortunately cannot go for Friday prayers. But I was lucky. Now I am working at the Muslim World League and we have a mosque attached to our office. So we pray *dhuhr*, and *jum'ah* and even *'asr* prayer.[7] Sometimes we even have evening prayers before we go home. But for other people in my area and for my family, our center is about forty-five minutes away. So on Fridays they barely go, pray and go back to work. It is hard. For other people it's hard to get permission to take off from work for Friday prayer. Some people can; some can't. But unless you have a center or a gathering of people or a house near where you work, it is difficult for people who work to come for Friday prayers.

EM: What do you think are the major issues that Muslims in North America and the world have to deal with as Islam moves towards the third Christian millennium and towards its own fifteenth century?

DA: Here is one example. When I got married in 1953, I was looking for a priest — well, we don't call him a priest; we call him an *imam* but you call him a priest here — to officiate at our marriage. I couldn't find any, except one who was in Brooklyn. I still remember the address: 43 State Street. It was the Islamic Mission. There was a fellow there from Ghana; his name — God bless his soul — was Dawud Faisal. He passed away about eight years ago. And I asked him, "Sheikh Dawud,

---

[7]*Dhuhr* is the obligatory noon prayer. *Jum'ah* is the Friday congregational prayer, which is usually observed in a mosque.

please come to our house to officiate at our wedding."
At that time I was in New Jersey. He said, "No, I cannot
go; you have to come here, to the mosque."

I said, "We have big family here, you know, about
twenty, twenty-five people."

He said, "I don't care; it has to be in the mosque."
So we had to come all the way up from New Jersey —
about fifty miles — to get married. Why? Because the
centers were few and Muslims were not too many.

But now I have on my list at least seven hundred or
seven hundred and fifty Islamic organizations or centers.
And there are maybe two or three hundred I don't even
know about. So Islam spread very fast in this period.
Nowadays, if you want to get married or you want to ask
a question about your problems, you will find in almost
every city, if not a center or an organization, at least a
gathering of people who will help. That's to show you
the best side of things.

But as a Muslim I also see the difficulties we have.
One thing that we worry about is our children. They are
the third generation. And they are actually "melted" in
this atmosphere. They don't know the Arabic language,
most of them. Or the Islamic religion. So we try to have
what we call "Weekend School." What you call Sunday
school. Sometimes Saturday; most of the time Sunday.
They go for two hours. Most of the centers have this.
One hour for Arabic language and one hour for Islam.

But this is not enough. Because at home, we've found,
the parents don't understand Islam. So it's difficult. You
have to teach the parents to teach their children. This is
one of the difficulties we are facing. In fact, our children
think that Palestine is Israel. They think Jerusalem is the
capital of Israel. So we try to teach them their history
and their religion and their language and their culture.

Educating our children is the major thing for us now.

So for the next fifteen years we are going to concentrate on having full-time schools for our children. In addition to the courses that the American curriculum requires, they will teach Islam and the Arabic language and the history of Islam. They will be boarding schools. So, we hope, the children will be familiar with their religion, their culture and their Arabic language.

EM: What do you see as some of the issues that Islam as a worldwide religion has to face?

DA: Well, the image of Islam now is not so good because of the Iranian situation, the war between Iraq and Iran, the Lebanese crisis and the Palestinians. Here the media are, I would say, very prejudiced against Islam. Either from ignorance or purposely, the media are influenced by the Zionists, or maybe it's our fault that we don't speak to the Americans in a language they understand. We are new to this country. We need people who can speak to the American people and mingle with their political system. PTA's — we should go there. And we should be part of the American environment, so that we can be known, like the Italians and the Spanish and others.

Once people understand about Islam — after we give them some material, the Qur'an and the Hadith[8] — a lot of people, especially educated people, say, "Well, we didn't know that Islam was that way." And a lot of people become Muslims, believe it or not. In Islam there is no compulsion in religion, but some people come here and they come to be Muslims. First I ask them why. If they tell me, "It's because my wife or my husband is a Muslim," I say that that's not enough. So I give

[8]See note, p. 8.

them some books and I tell them to come back after six months. If after six months they come back and if I know they are really serious, we explain to them the rituals and what they might face later on and so forth. Despite all this they become Muslims.

So things are changing now, especially after Elijah Muhammad passed away with his theories that black is dominant. Now Warith al-Din, his son, has changed the image of the black Muslims.[9] He himself graduated from al-Azhar[10] and he knows about the real Islam. They have come back to the true fold of Islam. They have started, for instance, to pray with us the same as we pray. They pass Ramadan in the same month we fast. They used to fast at Christmas time. And they used to call their mosques temples: Temple number 1, temple number 2, temple number 3. But now they call them mosque number 1, mosque number 2, mosque number 3. In fact, they change their names now to Arabic and Islamic names. And they come and start to teach Arabic. Because of people's desire to learn, we now have twenty-two full-time imams in our office, to explain the true Islam and to be leaders.

Because of the massacres that took place in Sabra and Shatila and the uprising now in Palestine and so forth, people start to study about the causes of this conflict. People start to have a sympathy for the Palestinians and sympathy for Islam. They say, "Well, it's not the same

---

[9]The movement of people who call themselves American Muslims has its roots in the nineteenth century. In the 1920s it developed as a protest by American blacks against white supremacy. In the last few decades, the movement has drawn closer to Islam as followed by the majority of its believers in the world. Warith al-Din is the present leader of this group, which maintains over two hundred mosques in the U.S.

[10]See note, p. 32.

image that we had before." I would say that for the last seven, eight or ten years we have been living in a prejudiced atmosphere. But now I see it's improving a bit.

We're going to concentrate on the media. We hope to have our own radio programs at least weekly and later on more often. To change the image. After all, we are in this country, we are American citizens and we should contribute to this country, to the quality of life.

EM: What do you wish North Americans knew about Islam? What do you want your non-Muslim friends and colleagues to understand about your religion from knowing you?

DA: I'm very glad that we have a dialogue between Muslims and Catholics, for instance, and other Christian religions. We have a dialogue between the Muslims and the National Council of Christians and Jews. We also have a National Council of Churches dialogue. We are co-communicating, and religious people are meeting together to understand each other. I feel this is a healthy sign, because if we, the religious leaders, do not come together to understand each religion and to help each other, we all suffer. This is a healthy sign and I encourage it.

And also I hope that peace will come to the Middle East. I feel that America has a lot to gain if it were a neutral party in the Middle East. Americans should not be one-sided, because they will lose their authority and their leading power. We would like to see the American government take a neutral position in the Middle East. It would be good for everybody. Now it's a one-sided story. We hope that in the future justice will prevail and peace will come to the Middle East.

7

Muhammad Halabi

Muhammad Halabi is a Ph.D. candidate in American Drama at New York University. A native of Syria, Mr. Halabi has taught English and American Drama at the University of Damascus, where he plans to return after the completion of his degree. Mr. Halabi is active in the cultural life of New York University and New York City. He is also working on an English translation of modern Syrian short stories.

Muhammad Halabi: I come from the coast of Syria, from a small town called Jabla. My home town has about twenty thousand people right now. And it's growing; we have two high schools. It's more like a village to me than

a town. The main landmark is an arena, a Roman arena.
And the town has about nine mosques.

I have been living in New York for three and a half
years. I'm pursuing a degree in Performance Studies at
NYU. Right now I'm in the middle of my course work
for the Ph.D. degree. Previously I got my M.A. from
NYU as well, from the English Department.

Elias Mallon: What will you do when you finish
your degree?

MH: I already have a job back at Damascus University teaching in the English Department and specializing
in drama, more specifically American Drama.

EM: Tell me a little about your family.

MH: There are eight of us. We are five children and
I'm the oldest son. I have three sisters and one brother.
And my grandmother lives with us. My father is a clerk,
an administrative clerk for religious affairs in the city. He
is the head of the department. My mother is a teacher
of drawing and sewing. My grandmother is illiterate.
She is the only member of the family who is illiterate.
My oldest sister is graduating this year from the English
Department at Tishrin University in Latakia. The middle
one got married two years ago and she is a civil engineer.
My little sister is a music teacher.

EM: Can you tell me some of the things that you
remember about Islam from when you were a child —
the earliest memories that you have of Islam?

MH: What terms of Islam are you talking about here?

Practice? Or are you talking about how did I learn more about Islam?

EM: Both.

MH: Well, my father used to take me to the mosque, as many fathers do. It is an obligation that a father take his son to the mosque. I was five or six. We lived near a mosque — it was just one or two minutes walk to the mosque. As for education, we had a course on Islam in high school and preparatory school. Until you graduate from high school there's education about Islam.

EM: And when would you start that — at what age?

MH: You start at the age of ten. And that means in elementary school, the last two years of elementary school. I still remember many of my teachers of Islam. There were many questions raised by the students. Many things in the course were not clear for the students. Every time we had class many students would come up with new questions. But a teacher can go only so far in explaining some things of Islam. There are miracles that we believe happened in the past and in the era of the Prophet. Sometimes the teacher would stop and smile at us. But you learn more from your life than from books if you live in a Muslim country.

EM: Was religion important in your family when you were growing up?

MH: I would say the practice of Islam is more important than "faith" in itself. If you're a Muslim you're supposed to fast during Ramadan, and if you don't, that means you're not a good Muslim. In these terms many

of my family — I would say all of them — do practice Islam. Definitely my grandmother — she prays five times
a day. But the new generation is not doing this any more.

EM: Not doing it at all? Or doing it differently?

MH: For example, instead of praying five times a day
they go only once for Friday prayer. And they think it's
enough. That's O.K. for them.

EM: That would be common now?

MH: Yes, for people from twelve to twenty-two.

EM: And older people?

MH: If you go to a mosque nowadays most of the
people in the mosque are old people. Very old. Like
fifties and older. They're there for every single prayer.
But as far as the youth in concerned, they are not sticking
to the practice.

EM: What about the middle group, between twenty
and fifty?

MH: It's either of two extremes, either to stick to the
practice fully or to abandon it. And that's because of the
pressures in the country.

EM: How is your identity as a Muslim expressed here
in New York differently from how it would be in Jabla?

MH: In a non-Muslim community, there are obstacles
if you want to stick to your identity or to stress your
identity. There is a kind of misconception of Islam in

this country. Many people that I've met only know the label "Islam." They don't know what Islam is. They only know what they pick up from the media. They see people praying on the ground and they assume that they're unclean or filthy. People practicing the prayer of Islam seem not as clean as clean-cut people who go to the church every Sunday. So you are stuck with that label. But this is a misconception about Islam. Cleanliness is part of Islam. If you pray every single prayer you have to wash for every single prayer.

Many people would assume from my name that I am a Muslim, and that has given me a hard time sometimes, many times. I've been denied a job just because of my name.

EM: We'll come back to that. Here in New York are you able to worship with other Muslims? And if so, in what kind of a setting?

MH: Yes, you can go and practice with other Muslims. There are many mosques in the city. I'm talking about the five boroughs. Mainly for Friday prayers. They're not open for prayer five times a day. But some of them in Brooklyn are, I believe, open five times a day. In most of those mosques they do insist that Muslims not stress Arab nationalism. Because being an Arab doesn't mean that you have to stress your identity as Arab. I've noticed that every time I go to Friday prayer most people try to uproot that kind of nationalism. "Don't be Arab; be Muslim."

EM: Is there a Muslim student organization at NYU?

MH: Yes. There is the New York University Islamic

Center. It has about a hundred members, but they don't get together for Friday prayer.

EM: Getting back to what you were talking about before. How have you been perceived as a Muslim or how is Islam perceived by non-Muslims that you know professionally or socially?

MH: As I said, from my first name you can pick up what religion I belong to. But there is a real dilemma for somebody who believes in his religion but tries not to stress it as far as society's concerned. For example, I have applied for different jobs, and I've been denied four or five. Just last week. One of them was open and nobody had applied for this job and the lady was trying to persuade me, "Muhammad, this is the job for you. You have that kind of résumé...." I set up the time for an interview. The guy seemed to be unhappy or uncomfortable with me. I expected to be denied. I called him back and he said they got somebody else.

EM: Have you any indication why that might be?

MH: Every time I gave my name I felt like they paused. Before I gave my name I was talking to them very comfortably. But when they asked for my name, my address, my phone number, I felt that pause as they spelled the name. This kind of pause gives me the impression that they're uncomfortable.

EM: So it's when you give your name. Among the students at NYU obviously a good number of your fellow students would know that you're a Muslim. What kind of a reaction do you get there?

MH: They do associate Islam with terrorism nowadays. It's known from the media that in the civil war in Lebanon different sects of Muslims are fighting each other. So they ask for some explanation — what's going on? How do you explain to me the militias? And the *hizbullah*?[1] Whatever. As far as Ramadan is concerned, they ask me how can I tolerate the fasting from dawn to sunset. Why am I doing this? Do I go to prayer? Just general questions. But I do have the impression that they're really open-minded.

EM: They would be open minded and curious?

MH: Oh, curious, of course. If somebody's practicing, they are curious about what's going on. Can you explain this or that?

EM: What about people in general, besides those you have dealt with recently for jobs. In other words, what are some of the North American stereotypes that you have to deal with?

MH: Terrorism.

EM: Terrorism. That has come up in many of the interviews.

MH: Right, right, I was expecting that. The "Muslim" — this term still seems vague to North Americans. They do know something about it. But they don't know the facts.

EM: What do they know or think they know?

---

[1]*Hizbullah*, Arabic for "Party of God," is a pro-Iranian faction in the Lebanese civil war.

MH: What I've seen through these years in North America is that Islam is associated with black people. Many people I've met are shocked when I tell them I'm Muslim because they associate Muslims with skin color.

EM: The black Muslims. Is it also the case outside New York that people think that Muslims are black?

MH: In major cities. Chicago, Los Angeles, but not in small cities. In New York City there's one thing a black person can mention: that Muslims in this city do have a kind of relationship regardless of skin color, culture, nationality. But when it comes to Arabic speakers and non-Arabic speakers, there is a difference. I have a feeling that non-Arabic speakers feel inferior because the Qur'an should be read in Arabic. And when you pray there's no way to pray in a translation. So there's a kind of clash, not a physical clash. They do feel a kind of inferiority. In the Turkish mosque where I usually go, we start the Friday prayer in Arabic but then we pray in Turkish. Otherwise those guys would be left out. There's no English. If you go to different communities, you will see some Arabic but still there's a kind of Arabic language barrier.

EM: In terms of your experiences both here in the United States and at home in Syria, what would you say that Islam has to deal with as we move towards the twenty-first century and the fifteenth century of the Hijra?[2]

MH: As we've seen lately in the Middle East, there is a kind of Muslim fundamentalist movement or under-

---

[2]The Muslim era, reckoned from the date of the emigration (*hijra*) of Muhammad from Mecca to Medina in 622 C.E.

ground organization, the Muslim brotherhood. It seems to me ironic that there where Islam was born it's oppressed. But here it's open. When it is open, there is misconception. Where it's oppressed, they do know the facts. Those people who live in North America don't know the facts and very few read books about Islam. In the Middle East the Muslim communities do practice Islam in a sense fully, but they are under great stress from their governments. They cannot do whatever they want to in terms of religion because there is no belief in the separation of state and religion. What really strikes me is that many Muslims in North America practice prayer differently from the way we practice back home. They follow different rules.

EM: What do you wish North Americans understood about Islam and your non-Muslim friends and colleagues understood about your religion from knowing you?

MH: I would like them to know that they should not associate Islam with Arabs. Islam is a religion. We do not discriminate between one culture and another, one color and another. Very few white Americans convert to Islam. The majority of converts are black. Black people have always been looking for a community to get them together to strengthen their ties. They thought that Islam, since it does not discriminate in skin color, would be a kind of asylum to them. I really think many of them feel happy when they come to prayer shoulder to shoulder with all different kinds of people. I've felt that kind of joy in them. Especially when after the prayer they go and shake hands and say, "May God accept your prayer." This is the typical expression that we use after prayer. So you feel then that they want to get closer to you but they don't know how.

8

Samer Hathout

*Samer Hathout is a student at the University of
California at Los Angeles. The daughter of two
medical doctors, Ms. Hathout is pursuing studies in philosophy. Although born in Kuwait, Ms.
Hathout has spent almost all her life in the United
States. Her hopes and dreams for her future are
similar to those of other young Americans. Her
Muslim faith, however, adds a different dimen-
sion to her approach to the world.*

Samer Hathout: My parents are from Egypt; both of
them are from Cairo. I was born in Kuwait and we came
to the United States when I was two. My grandparents
and most of my relatives are in Egypt, most of them in
Cairo.

Elias Mallon: Have you every visited them?

SH: Yes, I've been there a few times.

EM: Tell me a little about your family.

SH: My parents are both doctors from Egypt. They went to school in Egypt. I have one brother; he just finished medical school at UCLA.

EM: Obviously you learned the Muslim faith from your parents. But how have you grown in it as an adult?

SH: As I've gotten older I've learned a lot more and I've understood a lot more and I've studied a little bit more. And I think I have a much better understanding of the religion.

EM: What are some of your first memories of specifically Islamic things?

SH: Probably prayer. I remember my parents teaching me how to pray when I was pretty young. And we would pray together. I also remember fasting very well.

EM: How old were you when you started fasting for Ramadan?

SH: I started fasting at a pretty young age cause I really liked to do it. I thought it was a lot of fun. Maybe when I was ten years old.

EM: Fasting is so public. What kind of reaction did your schoolmates have?

SH: When I was younger they thought it was really neat. It was very hard to understand fasting from sunrise to sunset. They thought it would be very difficult to do.

EM: Have you gone to college?

SH: Yes, I'm in my second year.

EM: Is there any reaction there to your being a Muslim?

SH: No, not really.

EM: Any curiosity?

SH: There is curiosity about what Islam is because there are so many misconceptions.

EM: Could you explain some of the things that are part of Islam that have been very important to you, for example, in your family life?

SH: We pray together. And during Ramadan — a month of fasting, a very spiritual month, a holy month — we spend a lot of time together as a family.

EM: Describe a normal day in Ramadan.

SH: Well, usually all of us are gone until late in the afternoon. My parents are at work and I'm at school. Then we come home and pass the time until dinner. Then we break our fast and then we pray and then we have dinner. And then later in the evening we pray *tarawih*. It's a longer special prayer in the month of Ramadan and we pray it every night. And that's basically it. And then

there's school work. It's just a lot more spiritual time
and there's a feeling of peace in your heart.

EM: What do you do as a family for 'Id al-fitr?[1]

SH: We go to the Islamic Center for 'Id prayer. And
then we have breakfast together, and we visit friends.

EM: In your everyday life how is your identity as a
Muslim expressed, for example, at school? Where do you
go to school?

SH: UCLA. I'm a philosophy major.

EM: Any special direction of philosophy?

SII: No, not yet. I like ethical philosophy quite a bit.

EM: Would most of your friends know you're a Muslim, and how?

SH: All of my friends know I'm a Muslim. During
Ramadan they know that I'm a Muslim when I don't
have lunch with them. And they know my family and
they know I'm involved in the Islamic Center.

EM: Do you have a place where you pray at the university?

SH: Yes, we do have a room. The Muslim Students
Association.

EM: How many Muslim students are you in contact
with?

---

[1]See note, p. 32.

SH: Maybe thirty or forty.

EM: And how often do you meet?

SH: Usually just once a day.

EM: What about *dhuhr* and *'isha*?[2]

SH: Usually most of the people are home in time for *'isha*.

EM: Do you have any cousins your own age in Cairo?

SH: I have a few older than I am.

EM: How is your life in California different from theirs?

SH: I think it's more of a challenge to be a Muslim in North America just because we're a minority here. And not so in Egypt. Here it's not as common a thing to be a Muslim. When people ask me what religious faith I follow, they don't expect me to say I'm a Muslim.

EM: Do you encounter much curiosity?

SH: Yes, some.

EM: Any hostility?

SH: No, I haven't personally encountered any. No.

---

[2]*Dhuhr* is the obligatory noon prayer. *'Isha* is the closing prayer of the day for Muslims.

EM: Good. How often do you go to *jum'ah*[3] at the Islamic Center?

SH: Usually during the summer vacation and school breaks. Otherwise I go to find a prayer at school.

EM: There is Friday prayer at school?

SH: Yes, we do hold the Friday prayer at school.

EM: Is there a Muslim chaplain at UCLA?

SH: No, there isn't really a chaplain at all in the Muslim faith. But every week a different person gives the talk for Friday prayer. We do have a president of the Muslim Students Association.

EM: A student?

SH: He's a student, yes.

EM: How do you feel you are perceived as a Muslim? How is Islam perceived by non-Muslims that you know?

SH: I think there's a lot of confusion about Islam. People don't understand that it is a monotheistic religion and that it's part of the Judaeo-Christian realm. It should be called the Judaeo-Christian-Islamic realm. Because the beliefs are very similar.

EM: How do you think people see Islam?

SH: I think it's just misperceptions. They don't really know what Islam says or how Muslims worship.

---

[3]See note, p. 15

EM: When you tell someone you're a Muslim, immediately that forms an image in their head — either right or wrong — as to what you are. Do you have any stories about people who thought, well, she's a Muslim, therefore she must...?

SH: One thing I have, which doesn't really have anything to do with my being a Muslim, is my darker skin. Once someone came up and spoke to me. And you know how you speak to people when you think they don't know English? Very slowly, very loudly. He was very surprised when I answered him in English without an accent.

EM: Are there any North American stereotypes about Muslims that you're familiar with or you've personally had to deal with?

SH: Not that I personally have had to deal with. But there is the terrorist stereotype, that Muslims kill everyone. It's just not true. Islam is a religion of peace.

EM: Where would you experience this stereotype?

SH: It's mostly in the media. I haven't personally experienced this.

EM: Have you experienced any attempts to proselytize you on the part of Christians?

SH: I have had Mormons come to the door and just come in and talk to me.

EM: But that's more of an accident of where you are on the street. But you personally, specifically because you were a Muslim?

SH: No, never.

EM: What do you see as burning issues for Muslims in the U.S. and Canada? What are important issues for people your age that Islam has to deal with?

SH: Building an Islamic identity in a predominantly non-Islamic society. And just showing people that we are regular people.

EM: As you go into the professional world, how will you work to strengthen and spread your Islamic identity?

SH: Just practicing Islam in my daily life. Islam is a complete way of life. It isn't just prayer or fasting; it's kindness and hospitality and generosity. It's everything. Just being a good person I think is the best way to spread Islam.

EM: What do you think are the important issues for worldwide Islam? What do you think Islam is going to have to deal with in the next twenty or fifty years?

SH: Getting rid of the misconceptions is very important.

EM: And those misconceptions are...?

SH: Terrorism and inequality in the religion. I think those are the two basic stereotypes.

EM: What do you mean by "inequality in the religion"?

SH: People's misconception that men are better than women and other traditions that have come from other cultures.

EM: So this is an issue that you think that Muslims have to deal with?

SH: Yes. For non-Muslims, a knowledge about Islam.

EM: And for Muslims...?

SH: Working with the knowledge they have of Islam and gaining more knowledge of Islam to practice Islam.

EM: What about Muslim youth? What are their main concerns? What do they talk a about? What do they worry about?

SH: The main concern is building an Islamic identity, being accepted as a Muslim in the society.

EM: Do they feel they're not being accepted?

SH: Well, I generally felt that I was accepted.

EM: Do you notice any difference between your Muslim friends and your non-Muslim friends, especially at UCLA, in terms of the things that are important to them and the things they worry about?

SH: I would say so. The concerns of Muslims aren't so completely worldly. I mean, it would be true for any practicing Christian or any practicing Jew that your concerns aren't just with this world. There's more than making money or getting good grades. But this would be the same for anyone who practiced a religion.

EM: What do you think you as a young, North American Muslim woman can offer to the Islamic woman?

SH: Knowledge about the role of women in Islam. To understand that it is one of complete equality. Not to mix up the culture with the religion. That's a very important thing that I think women and men need to know about Islam.

EM: What do you hope that your non-Muslim friends and colleagues could understand about Islam from knowing you? In other words, what could they learn from you that they might not have learned from someone else?

SH: That Islam is a religion of peace and that it's a good religion and that Muslims are good people.

EM: What do you hope to do professionally with your life?

SH: Professionally, I haven't really decided yet. I'm always changing my mind. But I do want to do something professionally.

EM: I'm sure you're aware that there's a very rich Islamic tradition in philosophy. Do you have any opportunity to study that?

SH: I've seen one class offered. It's "Topics in the Philosophy of Islam."

EM: But you couldn't get a degree in Islamic philosophy from UCLA?

SH: No.

9

Mahmoud Mustafa Ayoub

Dr. Mahmoud Ayoub is a citizen of both Canada and the United States. After having studied and taught for several years in Canada, he is now Professor of Islamic and Religious Studies at Temple University in Philadelphia. Dr. Ayoub has an extraordinarily profound knowledge of Christianity and has done several important studies on points of spiritual contact between Christianity and Islam. He has also been active in interfaith work in Canada and the United States.

Elias Mallon: What are your ethnic and cultural origins?

Mahmoud Mustafa Ayoub: I am a Shi'ite born in south Lebanon, and so I'm an Arab from south Lebanon. I was born in a Shi'i family.[1]

EM: You said that you're from southern Lebanon. Could you describe the setting, the culture, the village that you came from?

MMA: Well, I was born in a small village in south Lebanon in the hills above Sidon, which was not so close to the border with Israel then. I grew up in that village. Because my parents were poor, and after I lost my sight as an infant, we moved to Beirut, the capital. There I went to a British missionary school for my early education. It was a Protestant kind of fundamentalist missionary school. So while I was born in a Muslim family, I had a Christian upbringing.

EM: Could you describe your education for us?

MMA: The school in Beirut was not much concerned with formal education but with religious and more specifically Christian education. So as I grew up and wanted to study more, I had to do it in a variety of ways — through correspondence and tutoring by university students and high school students and by reading. In 1957 I got a scholarship from the Perkins Institute for the Blind in Boston and the Ministry of Education in Lebanon, through the help of Mrs. Shamour, the wife of the president of Lebanon. I went to Perkins in Watertown, Massachusetts, where I finished my high school. I did it in one year. And I did a year of teacher training for the blind. Then I went back to Lebanon and eventually was

---

[1]See note, p. 5.

able to go to the American University of Beirut under an
A.I.D. scholarship. I graduated with a B.A. in philosophy
and a normal diploma of education in 1964. After that I
went to England. During my university years at Beirut I
got very interested in the Quakers, as I could no longer
regard myself as a fundamentalist Christian. But neither
could I see myself as a Muslim. So the Quakers provided
for me a kind of very nice period of transition. I went to
a Quaker school for about six months in England, after
which I was accepted at the University of Pennsylvania
here in Philadelphia, where from 1964 to 1966 I did a
Master's degree in religious thought.

Then I went to Harvard. My professor at Harvard at
the Center for the Study of World Religions was Wilfred
Cantwell Smith, a very committed, patriotic Canadian,
as he always described himself. And he noticed that my
knowledge of Islam, which is my tradition, was so scanty
that he suggested that I spend a year of special studies
at the Institute of Islamic Studies at McGill University
in Montreal. So I went to McGill in 1969 for a year
and took some courses to try to learn a bit more about
Islam. Then I went back to Harvard. At the time I got a
very good graduate fellowship from Kent and Danforth,
which allowed me to do some extensive travel in Iran
and the Indian subcontinent.

I spent a year in Toronto as a student of a priest of
the Pontifical Institute doing work in Passion literature,
medieval Passion literature. From this I developed my
thesis at Harvard, which I wrote on redemptive suffering
in Islam. I meant to do it as a comparative thesis between
Islam and Christianity, but the Islamic material was so
vast that I did it just on the Islamic side.

At Harvard I had a colleague who was a bit ahead of
me, Joe O'Connell, who then went to teach at the University of Toronto. He and another acquaintance worked

it out for me to go to Canada in 1978 as a visiting professor after I had taught for two years at San Diego State
University in California.

In Canada I got community funding to stay on as a research associate at the Center for Religious Studies at the
University of Toronto. I stayed there for about ten years.
I taught and did a lot of writing — books and articles.
And so I had a long Canadian experience, all together
about thirteen years. I taught for a year at McGill and
ten years at the University of Toronto. In Canada I got
married to a Canadian woman and have a family, two
children who were born in Canada. I took Canadian citizenship and lived as a Canadian. Last year there were
some political troubles — as always happens in academic
circles — so I did not get a position that was more or less
slated for me at the University of Toronto. I got instead
the position here at Temple. While teaching at San Diego
State University, I got my American citizenship as well in
order to bring some of my family here during the really
hard war years in Lebanon. So now I have dual citizenship — Canadian and American. I feel a lot of kinship to
both, really. I regard myself as a loyal Canadian as well
as a loyal American.

EM: How important was religion in your family while
you were growing up? Coming from a Shi'i family and
studying at a fundamentalist Christian school certainly
must have made for some tension.

MMA: Oh, a great deal of tension. My family — both
my parents — are very devout Muslims. They are not
educated. So for them being a Muslim means adhering
to all the principles and rituals of Islam. And of course
they wanted me to be a Muslim. And I wanted to save
their souls. So it created a lot of tensions. My father was

less sensitive to this than my mother. My mother always
said, "Leave him alone. He will return." It was only
when I came to study in North America as a graduate
student at the University of Pennsylvania, Harvard, and
the Canadian universities that I began to rediscover my
own religious and cultural roots.

My Christian upbringing has left an indelible mark
on my thinking. It's not that I have rejected Christianity,
but I feel that there is no one, single truth. I feel that my
cultural roots are really Middle Eastern and Islamic. But
my strong and close affiliation with Christianity gave me
something that most Muslims don't have, and that is the
ability to understand and to write and talk about Christianity in ways that Christians can understand. Even if
they don't agree, they can at least recognize this as the
way they also talk about their own tradition. So I have a
double personality here, religiously speaking. I am now
a practicing Muslim. I have a more mystical personal
approach to Islam. And I also see a great deal of beauty
in Christianity as well.

EM: In your everyday life how is your identity as a
Muslim expressed?

MMA: In a number of ways. First of all, I take Islam
seriously. That is to say, I do try to perform as regularly
as I can the five daily prayers, and fasting and so on.
I try in my own life and in my family also to observe
some — not all — but some of the dietary laws of Islam.
That is to say, I don't drink alcohol or eat pork. I try to
let my children know that they are Muslims. My nine-
year-old speaks Arabic and he knows by heart certain
portions of the Qur'an. I try not to be a bigoted religious person. Nor would I want to impose even on my
own children a strict kind of observance of Islam. I'd like

them to know who they are and make the decisions later on, as I have made them. In Canada I was quite active as a spokesperson for Islam, both in the media and in cultural and academic institutions. I was also quite active in the Muslim community in writing, lecturing and doing what I could to play my role as I see it as an educator. I am less political and have been less political than a lot of Muslims, and I feel that Islam has some lofty and good principles that somebody has to make sure are communicated somehow. And so I see myself really as an educator.

EM: In Canada you were able to worship with other Muslims?

MMA: Yes, there are in Toronto at least half a dozen mosques.

EM: Were you able to worship with other members of the Shi'a?

MMA: That is not an issue really. My Shi'ite identity is more or less a physical and cultural identity, but in my own approach to Islam I am non-sectarian. I don't regard myself necessarily as a Shi'i or Sunni Muslim. I try to adhere to the basic principles without bringing in all this sectarian conflict. It is not like Christianity where Protestants and Catholics have very different ways of worship. In Islam you can actually worship in any mosque. The differences are very minor, so that they do not affect the actual worship of the people.

EM: How do you feel you are perceived as a Muslim by non-Muslims whom you have worked with professionally?

MMA: I'm more accepted by them than I am by many of my Muslim brothers and sisters. They appreciate my emphasis on a pluralistic approach to the world. I regard Islam as a way of living, of worshiping, of relating to God and the world around me. I'm somewhat mystically inclined, really. Without being a member of any Sufi order,[2] my approach to Islam is highly mystical. That makes it easier for me to present Islam to non-Muslims than it is to present it to Muslims who want to look at things from very specific viewpoints. Anything that doesn't agree with their viewpoints is not right.

EM: Are there any North American stereotypes about Muslims that you've had to deal with?

MMA: Oh, yes, all the time. Canada is a good and civilized society; it's really an admirable society. Canada consciously sees itself as a multi-cultural society. By multi-cultural is meant multi-religious, multi-cultural, multi-lingual society. But often on the radio or in the local press there would be something very vicious against Islam and Muslims. I found myself often having to counter this, either through granting interviews or writing articles.

EM: Did you have any personal experience of that kind of behavior?

MMA: No. People were too subtle. The Muslim community is highly politicized. If I go to a particular mosque, for instance, I might not be easily accepted or welcomed. Shi'ites see me as not Shi'ite enough and

---

[2]The Sufis are a mystical movement in Islam. Sufis are found both among Sunni and Shi'i Muslims. They form groups or orders that follow the teachings of a spiritual leader.

Sunnis see me as Shi'ite. So I'm not accepted fully by either. Especially by establishment associations. But it doesn't bother me. I feel that maybe they are both correct. I'm not Shi'i enough or Sunni enough to fit into any stereotype.

There were certain government officials and media people who often stereotyped Arabs and Muslims, and for them the two were synonymous. Often one's political preferences — whether for Israel or for the Arab cause — determined whether one got support or ridicule. I and other Muslims have to deal with that. But because of Canadian law, which gives us a real chance, the situation is in a lot of ways better there than here. We had every right in Canada to stand up for our identity. We have it here, but here it's limited by all kinds of unspoken and sometimes loudly spoken ways that are accepted. You know, the films that are shown here, the stereotypes that are only beginning to change.

EM: Do you find a difference between the United States and Canada?

MMA: Yes, Canada is more compassionate as a society.

EM: What do you see as burning issues for Muslims in Canada and North America and for Muslims around the world?

MMA: These are both related and different issues. For the Muslim community in Canada and the U.S., one of the great problems is in some way to evolve its own identity that will be continuous with the Muslim community at large but that will also be different. That is to say, to see themselves as North Americans, living with

people who are not Muslims, going to school with them,
having non-Muslim neighbors and co-workers. To see
themselves as citizens of the U.S. and Canada, but also as
Muslims with definite sympathies and relations in their
home countries, whether it's the Arab world or Iran or
India or Pakistan. To find a balance between the two is
very important.

This sometimes gets to everyday issues. For instance,
the insistence of some Muslims that their boys and girls
do not meet often has meant in Canada that the boys,
who have a lot more freedom, have dated American or
Canadian girls and eventually married outside the community. For the girls, the family has often had to import
husbands for them from the home country. Girls born
or brought up in Canada often do not have anything in
common with young men from Pakistan or Egypt or Lebanon. So this is an issue that only a few communities in
the U.S. and Canada are beginning to grapple with. We
must realize that here boys and girls do meet. How can
we retain moral standards within which our young people can meet and even have fun and eventually let them
develop relations that lead to marriage? Some communities are beginning to deal with this.

Many problems will no doubt present themselves before the community finds its own feet in North America.
There are also political issues. Often the actual policies
of the country — the United States more than Canada —
are very antagonistic to a Muslim's country of origin.
The Arab-Israeli issue is one instance; the antagonism
towards Iran is another; the whole attitude of the governments toward Muslim countries is often a particular
political problem. And so, many Muslims find themselves with divided political loyalties.

My argument has been that there is no longer an en-
tity that we can call Dar al-Islam, the House of Islam.

Rather, the House of Islam must now be the homes, the hearts, the lives of Muslims wherever they are. And the Muslims who are in Canada, the U.S., Australia or Europe must live as good and loyal citizens of these countries, without completely assimilating and losing their Islamic cultural and religious identity. This is very difficult, because for most, practically all, Muslims in North America, there are three identities: there is their home in North America; there is the need for them to learn Arabic, which is the language of Islam, at least to the extent that they can pray and read the Qur'an; and then there is their loyalty to their own cultural origin.

We from the Arab world and the Pakistanis, for instance, have, very marked cultural differences. While we can get along in the mosque, our community activities must diverge because we have different cultural origins. And so there are all these problems that people have to deal with. And of course in Canada the Arab Muslims are a minority, a very small minority, compared to the Pakistanis and others. And so this becomes a problem. How do they relate? There are certain cities where there are sizeable Arab communities and these people relate to one another. But in the majority of situations, the Arab Muslims are a small minority. Of course there are many Arab Christians who are living now in Canada and the U.S. They have a great deal in common with Muslim Arabs, but the Muslim Arabs have to have a lot in common with non-Arab Muslims. There are these things that have to be worked out.

EM: What do you wish North Americans would learn about Islam from knowing you personally and from your writings?

MMA: I wish that North Americans would realize

that like Christian civilization — and that has a lot of different meanings — Islam is not monolithic. There is a tremendous diversity in the Muslim civilization, the Muslim community even today. And there is some unity. Islam is not only what the Iranians say, what the Indians or Pakistanis or the Egyptians say. But it is in some way what all of them say together. There is in my view that immutable Islam that is the principle of submission of all creation to God, unchanging, forever the same. It is for Muslims God's wish not only for humanity but for the entire creation; everything in the universe is *muslim* to God.[3] Only we human beings can make a choice either to affirm that commitment to live under God or to deny it. In affirming or denying there are all kinds of varieties.

I find it most problematic to say that all Muslims are backward because they dress in a certain way or they act in a certain way or they are violent. There is violence everywhere. There are national and cultural habits everywhere. And so all I try to do is show that there is a tremendous variety in Islam and that Islam is a very profound and beautiful spiritual civilization and heritage.

---

[3]See note, p. 24.